Finding
INTIMACY
in MARRIAGE

A Spiritual, Emotional and Physical Journey

Kim Hebenstreit

FAITH
BOOKS
MORE

Finding Intimacy in Marriage: A Spiritual, Emotional and Physical Journey

© Copyright 2014–Kim Hebenstreit

Unless otherwise noted, all Scripture quotations are taken from The HOLY BIBLE, NEW INTERNATIONAL VERSION ®. Copyright © 1973, 1978, 1984, by International Bible Society. Used by permission of Zondervan Publishing House. All rights reserved.

The "NIV" and "New International Version" trademarks are registered in the United States Patent and Trademark Office by International Bible Society. Use of either trademark requires the permission of International Bible Society.

First published by Faith Books and MORE, September 2014.

ISBN 978-1-939761-24-8

Printed in the United States of America.

No part of this book may be reproduced, stored in a retrieval system, or transmitted by any means without the express written permission of the author.

Graphic design by

3255 Lawrenceville-Suwanee Road,
Suite P250,
Suwanee, GA 30024
publishing@faithbooksandmore.com
www.faithbooksandmore.com

First and foremost, I thank my Savior.
You have given me every word of wisdom
and have redeemed my life.
You are my foundation.

To my husband, Woody, who has endured
my tears and fears throughout the years
You have taught me what it is to trust..
Your patience has endured my restlessness.
You truly are my only love.

Last, but not least, I want to express my deep gratitude
to my friend, mentor, and sister-in-Christ, Patti Johnson.
You have advised and listened with a heart full of love.
Thank you for every phone call, text, and email.
You are a gift from God.

I am a blessed woman.

TABLE OF CONTENTS

INTRODUCTION 1

1. WHAT DOES GOD HAVE TO DO WITH INTIMACY?................... 3
2. WHERE DO I START?... 11
3. RECOGNIZING THE THIEF... 21
4. WHAT IS PURITY AND WHY IS IT IMPORTANT?.................... 33
5. HOW THE THIEF DESTROYS.. 45
6. AN UNFORGIVABLE OBSTACLE: WHEN THE SIN IS NOT OUR OWN......... 57
7. ANOTHER BARRIER... 67
8. NOW WHAT?... 79
9. MAKING ALL THINGS NEW 89
10. BUILDING ON SPIRITUAL INTIMACY................................ 103
11. AN EMOTIONAL BOND.. 117
12. PHYSICALLY FIT FOR INTIMACY.................................... 129

INTRODUCTION

I believe I have spent my entire life searching for intimacy—intimacy with my parents, my siblings, my friends, and eventually, my husband. I had a yearning for something deeper than what I was experiencing in my life. I needed to experience an undeniable connection with another human being that left me feeling completely fulfilled and necessary. A feeling of purpose, the feeling that someone could look deep into my soul and understand my innermost desires, that is what I was seeking. My quest took me in many different directions and was the motivation behind many of the regretful choices I have made throughout my life.

I would love to say that when I entered into a personal relationship with Jesus Christ, the longing for intimacy with another human being dissipated, but it didn't. Then, more than ever, I felt the need to connect with other like-minded individuals to share my newfound joy. I longed to share my love for Christ with my husband so that we could connect on a whole new level. Unfortunately, he did not share my enthusiasm, and for nearly five years he despised the intimacy I had with Jesus Christ. He considered my relationship with God to be an adulterous relationship. He was fearful of being replaced in my heart by a spiritual being that he wasn't even sure existed. Again, I found myself searching for intimacy; this time with my husband.

My husband did eventually come to have a saving faith in Jesus Christ as his Savior and has since taken giant leaps in his spiritual growth. He is a wonderful leader and has led our family faithfully for many years. However, his newfound faith did not bring an end to our problems in connecting intimately—spiritually, mentally, and physically. My journey was not finished; it had just begun. Once again, I was searching for intimacy, but this time with God as my guide.

The Bible shows us the history of relationships. It is also a love letter demonstrating the deepest, most intimate bond in a relationship. As we move forward on this incredible voyage, ask God to reveal to you His will for your relationship with your husband. Jeremiah 29:11 tells us that God knows the plans He has for you. He has *"plans to prosper you and not to harm you."* Isn't that what we need, God to prosper our marriages? God's will is to breathe new life into your marriage and move it to a level you never imagined was possible. You are about to embark upon what may be one of the most difficult expeditions you have ever encountered. But once the destination has been reached, you will be rewarded by a more intimate relationship with God, with others, and most importantly with your spouse. It is God's desire for your life. With Him leading the way and shining His light upon your path, you will be rewarded with what many married couples have desired at some point during their lives—to be more personally connected with their spouses -one of the most important relationships they will ever have.

I realize that for most, this is likely a very frightening journey upon which to embark. It means facing aspects of your life that you may not want to encounter. I understand. Satan had me completely immobilized by fear for nearly two years. It wasn't until my dissatisfaction with "status quo" was greater than my fear that I was willing to do whatever it took to change my marriage. I was in such a dark place. I could find joy with everyone except my own husband. Woody knew this. He constantly asked me why I was so unhappy, to which I could never give an honest answer. How could I tell him, "I hate what our marriage has become." It wasn't until I was on the brink of destruction that I was willing to face my fear and overcome it with God's divine strength.

Facing my past (which is littered with more trash than I care to mention) was *not* something I wanted to do. Yet God made it quite clear I had to face it in order to leave it behind me. I realized that I was constantly looking over my shoulder at what was behind me instead of looking forward to what might be. It was a long process—a painful process—but I am so very glad I finally took the bull by the horns and confronted every deep dark secret that stood between me and the intimacy which God had planned for me to experience with my husband. Afterwards, I could actually say "wonderful husband," which was not an adjective I would have used before my journey.

Change is never easy, especially when it requires digging through our closets and revealing the skeletons we have hiding there. However, God's amazing ability to bring healing and restoration is waiting. He makes **all** things new. Imagine how grateful I was when I realized that meant me too! He has purified me in a way in which I could not even fathom. I am no longer looking over my shoulder waiting for the past to catch up with me and steal my contentment. It is over. All of my sins have been thrown into the deepest trench in the ocean, and I am never going fishing there again!

CHAPTER 1

WHAT DOES GOD HAVE TO DO WITH INTIMACY?

I was not raised in a Christian home; therefore, when I was searching for a husband, I really didn't see what God had to do with the decision making process. I knew enough to know that I shouldn't be "unequally yoked," but beyond that I didn't see where He fit into the plan. Surely God did not have any ideas about intimacy, at least, not what I envisioned that association to be. Unfortunately, like many people today, I equated sex to intimacy; and as far as I was concerned the Bible was a list of "do's" and "don'ts" when it came to the subject of sex.

The real issue at hand was that I did not have an intimate relationship with God. He was a distant spiritual entity that I didn't want to anger for fear of being struck by lightning. Although I had been to church as a child and had a wonderful knowledge of the Bible's stories, I did not have an understanding of the church's views on intimacy since this was not taught during the primary grades. I did know that God loved me and desired to have a relationship with me; I just didn't know what that required on my part.

It is hard to understand what our relationships with others are to look like until we have a personal relationship with our creator God. Until we have crawled into His loving presence and have experienced His grace, we cannot fully comprehend what it means to completely trust without fear of rejection. Until we have experienced His unconditional love, it is virtually impossible to understand true intimacy. Unfortunately, this all-consuming knowledge of God did not happen until after I was married.

To say our relationship suffered much during the first several years of our marriage is an understatement. I was a brand new, recommitted Christian, and my husband was somewhat Gnostic. He believed in a God; he just wasn't sure how personal or real that "God" should be. To complicate matters, we had had a child before our nuptials. To start off a marriage with a child and unequally yoked had definitely not been God's plan.

During my first year of marriage, I began to feel God's loving presence as He wooed me back into a committed relationship with Him. I fell "head over heels" in love with our wonderful Creator and everything in my life took on a new appearance. God transformed my ideas as to the type of wife and mother I should be. The journey, nonetheless, would prove to be difficult and full of obstacles, with the biggest obstacle being my pride.

I praise God that during this time Woody was patient and stayed the course. The new Christian I had become was judgmental, stubborn, and self-righteous. Woody's every action came under my scrutinizing gaze. If he did anything that I deemed "un-Christ-like," I was the first to notify him of it. Our relationship did not grow closer as it should have. My faith had put a wedge between us. God slowly changed my heart, and as I matured I saw my sin of pride for what it was. My stubbornness became submission; my judgmental, self-righteousness became humility. I learned to bite my tongue and let God deal with Woody's heart. Regrettably, the damage had been done in my relationship with Woody. We had become so emotionally distant that I didn't know how to traverse the expanse that separated us.

It was during this time that I came to the realization that intimacy has absolutely nothing to do with sex and everything to do with a spiritual connection. God has everything to do with intimacy. He created us to have an intimate relationship with our spouses. Somehow during the course of history, we have skewed the definition of intimacy that God has planned for His children. The first step in regaining that closeness is understanding God's plan for marriage and how God is intricately involved in our relationships. Read Genesis 2:8-25.

In verse 18 what does God say is not good for man?

 _____

_____

WHAT DOES GOD HAVE TO DO WITH INTIMACY?

God immediately recognized Adam's need for companionship—that it was not good for man to be alone. God had brought all of the animals to Adam, but Adam had not been able to find a companion comparable to him.

Genesis 2:23

The man said,

"This is now bone of my bones
and flesh of my flesh;
she shall be called 'woman,'
for she was taken out of man."

In verse 23 what does Adam recognize immediately concerning his relationship with the woman?

╰╼ _____

_____

_____

Adam immediately realized that Eve was a part of him, the intimate connection was made.

What does it mean to you to be "one flesh?"

╰╼ _____

_____

_____

There is an intimacy in becoming "one flesh" that we have become unaware of in today's society. Over 3,000 years have passed since the words in Genesis were recorded, and we no longer understand the tender familiarity that should take place between a husband and a wife when they become "one flesh." It should be a sweet mystery to be discovered within the protective bonds of marriage.

Verse 25 reads, *"The man and his wife were both naked, and they felt no shame."* I love that visual! To stand before each other, completely exposed, vulnerable in every sense and to experience no shame, no threat of wrongdoing by the other, to completely trust!

Have you ever stood in front of your husband completely naked, literally and figuratively? If you have never been able to stand before your husband utterly defenseless in your nakedness, what has prevented you from doing so?

༄ _____

_____

_____

_____

Marriage was created on the sixth day in the Garden of Eden. God's plan was for a man and a woman to become one and in doing so, stand unashamed before Him and each other entirely stripped of all pretenses, trusting, loving, and knowing. We can't genuinely know another until we have stood before him without any barriers blocking our view.

Now, read Genesis 24:62-66. This is the story of Isaac and Rebekah. Rebekah was an answer to prayer. She went willingly with Abraham's servant away from all that she loved and knew to marry a man whom she had never met. All she truly knew was that he was a man of God. In this passage we are invited to take a glimpse into that first meeting. We see Rebekah climbing down from her camel and covering herself. You can almost picture Isaac taking her in, realizing God's choice for his life. And then verse 66 says it all, *"he married Rebekah…and he loved her; and Isaac was comforted after his mother's death."* She was his comfort, his love, his answer to prayer. He took her into his tent without any shame, without any deception. They became one flesh and completely understood what it meant to be in a covenant, intimate relationship with a spouse.

Again, we see God's plan for intimacy in a marriage. We should be comforted and loved. Exposed and trusting. These two passages do not even begin to encompass all that God has planned for us as His children. How excited I was to discover God's purpose for my marriage! He has the same plans for you and your marriage. Think on that for a moment…God wants you to find love, trust, and comfort. Do you trust God to fulfill His intentions for your marriage? If not, ask Him now to give you the faith to know He is a God of purpose and promise.

"Thank you, Lord, for your unfailing love.
Thank you for planning my life and letting the
union with my spouse be a part of Your plan.
Help me to trust Your goals for my marriage.
Let me feel Your loving presence within my home,
constantly holding me up and reassuring me.
In Jesus' holy name I pray. Amen"

My Journal
continuing the journey...

date _____

CHAPTER 2

WHERE DO I START?

I've always said that head knowledge is different than heart knowledge. When I finally realized God's definition of intimacy in a marriage, I didn't have any idea how to apply my new found wisdom. And although God had made me aware of His plan for marriage, when was He going to let my husband in on the good news? Woody by this time had accepted Christ as his savior but was taking baby steps in his new walk. I wanted desperately to grab him by the hands and drag him down the path so that he might catch up with me. I was not patient with his growth. I wanted him to mature yesterday. Why was it taking so long? Didn't God know I wasn't good at waiting? I kept asking over and over, "Now what?" I didn't realize that the next step would be the most painful and the most introspective. I didn't realize that I was the one whose heart God would be working on.

More than anything I longed to bridge the divide between Woody and me. I longed for that familiarity that would cause us to be one, spiritually, emotionally, physically. I longed to open up my soul to my husband and know that I need not be ashamed or fearful. I needed to feel his adoration and respect. I needed his unconditional love. How in the world would I even begin to acquire all that I longed for?

I realized that it was hopeless for me to reach the place God wanted me to go in my marriage on my own. God's ideal was so far from anything I recognized or knew. It had not been modeled for me by my own parents. Brokenness is what I had seen growing up. Lives lived outside the will of God, that's what I was familiar with. How would a young woman from a broken family with a sinful past behind her ever come to know such perfect love? It was too late for me, I was sure. We had already defiled the marriage bed. We had already picked the fruit before it had become ripe and now it had spoiled. How could God ever bless such a marriage!

Once again I found myself on my knees and searching God's Word for the answers that I so desperately sought.

God is so patient. My story was the story of every Christian. We love a perfect God. We are a wicked and perverse people. We picked the forbidden fruit all those years ago and continue to do so. We've spoiled the sweet life that He had planned for us. We have brokenness and sinfulness lying in the path behind us. How could God ever bless us? And yet He did through the most amazing gift He ever bestowed upon us, His son, Jesus Christ! It wasn't too late for me while I was yet a sinner, and it isn't too late for me now. Just as every sinner has to come to the place where he or she recognizes his or her own inability to cleanse himself and make himself whole, I had to come to the same recognition within my marriage. I had to trust that God had made a way, and that He would reveal that way to me.

I knew paradise was waiting, but God would have to lead me on the journey and reveal to me the course to take. As I delved into His Word, I wasn't sure where to begin. I lugged my exhaustive concordance off the shelf and placed it on the table before me. "Okay, God. I guess I'll start with the word marriage. I really don't know what else to look for, but I'm trusting You'll make it clear." I discovered that for the word marry and its various forms, there are over 80 entries in the "Strong's Exhaustive Concordance of the Bible." I started the exhausting work of reading every passage in context that had to do with marriage, and that was truly when my voyage to healing and restoration began. I discovered that the "quick fix" I was hoping for was going to be a prolonged process. There wasn't one Bible verse to read and memorize, or one attitude I needed to adjust. It would take time, trust, and coming face to face with the truth of my past. Which brings us to the next question on our journey; "What does my past have to do with my present?"

What does my past have to do with my present?

Exodus 21 was one of the first places I was led to on my investigation of the word marriage. Now, I have to admit, although I had read through the book of Exodus in the past, there were a few chapters that I had skimmed over, especially those concerning the Mosaic Law. I knew chapter 21 was one of those chapters. It was the law concerning servants, and I was quite certain that it was not applicable to my life. Yet, there I was staring at Exodus 21:8. For some reason I could not move past that verse. I read it and reread it. I read the whole chapter. I read chapter 20. I wanted to ensure that I wasn't taking anything out of context. Still, I could not understand why God kept leading me back to that one verse. I even read several translations. It didn't change the meaning, nor did it give me any more insight. The New King James Version is as follows: *"If she* [the female servant that has been purchased] *does not please her master, who has betrothed her to himself, then he shall let her be redeemed. He shall have no right to sell her to a foreign people, since he has dealt deceitfully with her."*[1]

On the surface, I knew that this was a law concerning a man who purchased a female servant, and how the situation was to be handled if he broke contract with her. But in my spirit I also knew that God was trying to communicate something more to me. I kept asking, "How has he dealt deceitfully with her? No, he didn't keep up his end of the bargain, but what else? If he is not pleased, is it because he is in the wrong?" That's when it hit me like a train crashing into my thoughts; how often do our past deceptions cause us to find no joy in our present circumstances? Do we deal deceitfully about our past and then become discontented with our present? Now, I'm not saying that that's what this verse is speaking about, but that's the message God gave me in that moment. I realized that my past was affecting my present, robbing me of the abundant life God has in store for all of His children. But what could I do? I could not change my past.

Our first step in becoming followers of Christ is acknowledging that we are sinners. Only after we come to the understanding that we are hopeless to save ourselves do we begin to comprehend God's grace. When we realize our failings, we begin to see His redeeming love for what it is. We find fulfillment in His restoring love. Although I had been forgiven for my past transgressions, I was still carrying them around, lugging them into all of my relationships. Some of them I hadn't really dealt with, not recognizing them for what they were. I carried them in my memories and in my dreams, asking questions such as, "What if...?" Although God had sealed up my sins in a bag and had thrown them into the

---

[1] *The Holy Bible, The New King James Version*, (Thomas Nelson, Inc., Nashville, 1999), p. 69

deepest ocean, I had gone out fishing and had opened up the bag to play with a few of them. I was standing in the way. I was the biggest obstacle in the road that led to the intimacy I yearned for. In order for me to grow and find joy, I needed to contend with my past—face it down and overcome it; acknowledge my sin for what it was—separation from God. Only then could I travel into the future that God has in store for all who are His.

I realized the sins from my past were robbing me of future joy. Because I had memories of past relationships, it was easy for me when experiencing a difficult situation with Woody to grab onto those memories and seek comfort in them, deluding myself with dreams of what my life might have been.

Is there anything in your past, whether failed relationships or other lifestyle choices, that keeps popping up in your present preventing you from experiencing contentment? What do you ask, "What if…" about? List those things now.

If you made a list, is there anything that you have not sought God's forgiveness for? Or do you have things on the list that you have repented of but have not yet accepted God's forgiveness for? If so, write those things below.

෪ _____

_____

_____

_____

_____

Read Micah 7:18-20.

Micah 7:18-20

[18] Who is a God like you,

    who pardons sin and forgives the transgression

    of the remnant of his inheritance?

  You do not stay angry forever

    but delight to show mercy.

[19] You will again have compassion on us;

    you will tread our sins underfoot

    and hurl all our iniquities into the depths of the sea.

[20] You will be true to Jacob,

    and show mercy to Abraham,

  as you pledged on oath to our fathers

    in days long ago.

According to verse 19, what does God do with our sins?

God does not hold on to our past mistakes. He delights in mercy! Your failings have been cast into an abyss. Past relationships, whether good or bad, have no place in your marriage. Throw them away!

I want you to take a black Sharpie and mark through your lists. God did the moment you confessed; now it is your turn. Quit highlighting your transgressions. They are not worth remembering. Those things will only bring misery and regret into your present situation and continue to steal from you the joy God has waiting for you. Look now to your present with hope for the future.

*"Lord, You are forgiving and merciful!
You alone can erase the effects of choices made
outside of Your will. You can bring healing
and freedom. Thank you for your gift!
In Jesus' name I pray. Amen."*

My Journal
continuing the journey...

date _____

CHAPTER 3

Recognizing the thief

Exodus 21 made it quite clear to me that one of the first steps on the journey toward complete intimacy is recognizing the thief. We have to question, "What is it in my past that is robbing me?" We cannot fight the enemy if we do not recognize him for whom or what he is.

It is so easy to go through life with blinders on. Or perhaps it is merely a lack of recognition. "I haven't done anything wrong. Sure, I may have experimented with sex before marriage, but who hasn't? I had lots of relationships and learned something valuable from each one. What's the big deal?" You may feel as if the choices you made and the experiences you had have nothing to do with your current struggle for intimacy.

I grew up in the late 70s and early 80s, post-sexual revolution. My mother never spoke to us about sex other than to tell us it was a "very evil" thing to engage in. When we were taken to church, we heard the same thing; yet the message I received from the media and my peer group was, "sex is great!" Free love! That's what it's all about. "If you can't be with the one you love, love the one you're with." To say I was conflicted is an understatement. And of course the first time I kissed a boy, I quickly realized that my mother and the church had no idea what they were talking about. If kissing felt that good, then sex had to be even better. Since no one could explain to me why sexual intimacy before marriage was wrong other than "the Bible says so," I lost no time at all in formulating my own ideas of acceptable sexual behavior. Surely there could be nothing damaging in having fun as long as I didn't "go all the way." Even some of my church going friends agreed with my sentiments

I have come to the realization that in our society there are many diverse ideas as to what defines sexual immorality, even among Christians. The sexual revolution changed our thoughts concerning accepted ideas on sexuality. It was a time of de-conditioning from old-world ideas and values that were rooted in Christianity. The idea of "free love" in the 1960s and into the 1970s brought about great change in sexual experimentation, such as open sex in and outside of marriage. Contraception, public nudity, legalization of abortion, "no-fault" divorce, and the decline in religious observances as westernized cultures pulled away from Judeo-Christian traditions can all be attributed to the sexual liberalization of our country. We no longer have a Biblical idea as to what sexual morality is.

If we were to believe what our media driven society has spoon fed us over the past 30 to 40 years, we would be under the impression that none of our actions—especially when it comes to sexual freedom—have consequences. We would also believe that sex is never immoral when it is consensual. At the beginning of the sexual revolution in 1961, a young girl told Esquire magazine that, "I used to think it was terrible if people had intercourse before marriage. Now I think each person should find his own values."[2] And that is what we have done as a society in general; we have found our own values. The consequences of unprotected sex have been removed one by one. We have contraception, penicillin, vaccines against the human papilloma virus, and more. Sex is good! So, as long as both parties are in agreement, who or what does it hurt?

What does God say is sexually immoral?

We know what constitutes sexual immorality in our culture—nothing! So, what does God say is sexually immoral? And how relevant is the teaching of the Bible? I mean, really, aren't Paul's ideas antiquated? Seriously, he really didn't face the same moral issues that our culture is faced with. Or did he?

When Paul wrote about sexual immorality in his letters, he confronted many of the same ideas concerning acceptable sexual behavior as we do today. Sexual immorality is not new. Ancient Greece and Rome had sexual and moral codes very similar to what we have today. Greek and Roman gods were known to

---

[2] David Boroff, "Among the Fallen Idols, Virginity, Chastity and Repression," *Esquire*, July 1961, p.98

lust after and even rape each other. Temple prostitutes were the norm as was homosexuality. Bestiality and sadomasochism are not new to this millennium. We can trace some of these practices back to ancient civilizations. In fact, according to some sources, chastity was considered to be an impossible standard during the first century, which is the time period in which Paul wrote his letters.[3] So when Paul said, *"Flee sexual immorality. Every sin that a man does is outside the body, but he who commits sexual immorality sins against his own body,"*[4] he wasn't uninformed or naïve. He was well versed in what sexual immorality was and is.

Paul knew what God knows and what we need to know. When we engage in intimate relationships, we are forever changed. The people that we have invited into our hearts leave an imprint that does not go away when they do. The truth of the matter is there is no such thing as "free love." It's simple physics—for every action there is an equal and opposite reaction. Everything has a price! And I don't know about you, but my choice to become sexually active before marriage has not given me feelings of liberation; instead, I feel imprisoned by memories and regrets. There was a cost. The price was high. We cannot indulge our senses without being impacted in some way. Every life experience affects us positively or negatively. Unfortunately, sexual intimacy outside of the beautiful bonds of marriage will never have overall positive consequences. Physical "love" is not free.

I love the King James Version best of Romans 1:21-32. It is, in my opinion, the best literal translation of what Paul was trying to communicate to the Roman church about sexual immorality and man's fall into it. It so well describes what happened to our culture during the sexual revolution. Man exchanged the idea of God and all His old-fashioned ideas for a new, modern view in which man is god of his own universe and his own destiny. In verse 28, we see that *"even as they did not like to retain God in their knowledge, God gave them over to a reprobate mind, to do those things."* If we continue to read in verse 29, we see that the results of this were *"all unrighteousness, fornication, wickedness, covetousness, maliciousness;"* and the list goes on and on.[5] The word used for "fornication" in this passage is the Greek work, "πορνεία," or "porneía." It

---

[3] *The NIV Study Bible, 10th Anniversary Edition*, (The Zondervan Corporation, 1995), p. 1825, Study Notes, 1 Thessalonians 4:3
[4] 1 Corinthians 6:18
[5] *KJV Compact Reference Bible*, (The Zondervan Corporation, 2000), p. 1276

includes all forms of sexual immorality.[6]

Porneía is very broad in its meaning; so much so that some have tried to insinuate that premarital sex is not included in the definition. However, a close look at God's ideal reveals that what we have come to accept as sexually moral behavior doesn't even come close. In fact, we are not even in the same ball park. In order to understand just how far off the mark we are, we will need to go back to the Garden of Eden where marriage was first instituted by God.

In Genesis two, we discover that Adam, although surrounded by creatures of every kind, was lonely. I can only imagine what it must have been like. Here he was in the most beautiful, romantic garden of all times and he had no one of equal status to share his newfound discoveries. God knew this would happen. He had placed within Adam a longing for companionship—the foundation of all relationships. He caused Adam to fall into a deep sleep, took one of his ribs, and formed a stunning woman from the same materials He had used to make Adam. You can just about picture Adam's surprise when he awoke to this gorgeous, naked woman who not only was similar to Adam in form, but also could communicate on the same level. "Ah, flesh of my flesh! She will be called woman." And as they consummated their relationship, they became one. They were married—no ceremony, no license; just God's blessing. The physical act is what instituted the union of marriage. In Genesis 2:24, we read: *"For this reason a man will leave his father and mother and be united to his wife, and they will become one flesh."*

If you fast forward through the book of Genesis, you will find the story of Isaac and Rebekah. In chapter twenty-four, we discover that Abraham's chief servant went in search of the perfect woman for his master's son, Isaac. Rebekah was the answer to his prayers. When the servant returned to Canaan with Rebekah, Isaac was out in the field meditating. At the same time Isaac saw the servant approaching with the lovely Rebekah, Rebekah noticed him and made inquiries. When she discovered it was her husband to be, she covered herself with her veil (a sign of her virginity). Isaac made his way to the small group and was informed of all that had occurred. This maiden was to be his wife. What happened then? Did they have a time of courtship while planning a lavish wedding? No, because in that time period a ceremony did not constitute marriage. Genesis 24:67 tells us *"And Isaac brought*

---

[6] James Strong, Strong's Exhaustive Concordance of the Bible: With Greek and Hebrew Dictionaries, (Dugan Publishers, Inc.), p. 59.

her into his mother Sarah's tent, and took Rebekah, and she became his wife."[7] That was it! When a man had sexual relations with a woman, he entered into a binding, covenant relationship that could not be undone. It was what Jesus was referring to in Matthew 19:3-6. This is the union that makes us one. Sex is marriage.

As time went on, strict laws governing marriage were put into place, some ordained by God, others by man. The common theme, however, is that sex before marriage was never condoned by God. In fact, in the Hebrew culture it was virtually impossible to have premarital sex. If a man did have sex with an unwed, unattached virgin, he was required to marry her and could not ever divorce her (Exodus 22:16; Deut. 22:28-29).

God's Word indicates that He takes sex seriously. Peruse the books of Exodus and Deuteronomy and you will find laws concerning whom you may have sex with and when. This is not to be taken lightly. God knew we would pervert this wonderful gift that He had given to man during creation in the Garden of Eden. He also knew that by abusing His gift, we would not only corrupt our relationships with others, but we would also damage our relationship with God.

However, the most debilitating aspect of corrupting God's plan for sex has been the break down of understanding the church's relationship with God. We are more likely to understand the "mystery" of Christ's relationship with the church if we can understand the intimacy of marriage and how God designed it to be. There is a connection in becoming one flesh of which we have lost sight since the sexual revolution. Unfortunately, we no longer truly understand what forming an inseparable union looks like. If marriages cannot be trusted, then how can we trust God? And if we do not know what it looks like to be "one" physically, how can we be "one body" spiritually?

God has, and has always had, a perfect plan for His children. He does not put rules into place to take the fun out of life for us. He does so to protect us from the things in life that He *knows* will harm us. Even when He gave the Israelites all of those rules in Exodus and Deuteronomy concerning sexual relationships (you know—the ones we love to skim over without serious contemplation), He was safeguarding the women in a patriarchal society. Nothing escapes His notice. He knows human

---

[7] *KJV Compact Reference Bible*, (The Zondervan Corporation, 2000), p. 29

nature and the tempter *intimately*. Therefore, He has given us all the information we need to establish loving relationships with each other and with Him. That is His ultimate plan! To be in relationship with His most cherished creation—you!

Maybe you understand that premarital sex is forbidden in God's Word, and you might agree that, because of this, one could make the argument that it is immoral. Nevertheless, you still may not see why it is important to remain pure before marriage or how it is related to intimacy; you have yet to recognize it for the thief it is. Or possibly, you were "technically" a virgin when you married. You could have been one of those who truly believes as long as you don't engage in intercourse, you are remaining pure. Therefore, this could not possibly be the problem.

This thief is nearly unrecognizable as it prances through our society as a glorified celebrity rather than the destructive criminal it truly is. Our culture's lack of purity and our nonchalant approach to sex are cheating our relationships of true intimacy. We have turned God's plan completely upside down as we try to build spiritual and emotional intimacy on top of physical affection. We fail to perceive how our past behavior influences our present situation. But whether we acknowledge it or not, the damage has been done with or without our consent.

Before I address the idea of God's standard of sexually moral behavior even further in the next chapter, let's take another look at God's Word for what He says about sex before marriage. Read Exodus 22:16 and Deuteronomy 22:28-29.

Exodus 22:16

[16] "If a man seduces a virgin who is not pledged to be married and sleeps with her, he must pay the bride-price, and she shall be his wife.

Deuteronomy 22:28-29

[28] If a man happens to meet a virgin who is not pledged to be married and rapes her and they are discovered, [29] he shall pay the girl's father fifty shekels of silver. He must marry the girl, for he has violated her. He can never divorce her as long as he lives.

Did men have the option of having casual sex with unmarried women?

ಎ _____

_____

_____

Now read 2 Samuel 13:1-20.

This is the story of Tamar, a beautiful daughter of King David. Her half-brother, Amnon, lusted after her to the point he thought it was love.

What does Tamar say to her brother in verse 13 about his desire to have premarital sex with her?

ಎ _____

_____

_____

_____

Before he raped her, Tamar begged Amnon to go to the king and ask for her hand in marriage. She most likely knew that this was forbidden by law (Lev. 18:9; 20:17), but in the moment, she was merely trying to avoid his advances.

What does Tamar say to Amnon in verse 16 after he has violated her?

ಎ _____

_____

_____

_____

Tamar knew that she would no longer be eligible for marriage. Her virginity had been defiled. She was a ruined woman.

How does this compare to today's view of a woman who has sex before marriage?

✍ _____

_____

_____

_____

_____

How did we get to the point where we can use "casual" and "sex" in the same sentence, let alone use casual as an adjective to describe sex? If you look in a thesaurus, one of the antonyms listed for the word "casual" is "designed." Casual sex is the exact opposite of what God designed!

We have spoiled God's plan so much so that we no longer recognize sin for what it is. We have become desensitized to the point that we rationalize, justify, and teach our sinful behavior as being morally desirable. After all, you wouldn't buy a car without test driving it; and how will you know if you are sexually compatible if you don't experiment beforehand? We are so far from the truth that finding our way back has become painfully difficult. We really do not want to face the reality of our own sin. We would rather take the world's view because then we don't really look that bad.

Denial does not free us—it traps us in a vicious cycle that we can never escape. We must face our iniquities head on with God's help in order to break free. Then, and only then, can we move toward God's healing and restoration.

"Father God, facing my sin is painful. It is so hard to look upon past behavior as morally reprehensible. I don't want to admit that my indiscretions were wrong. I enjoyed myself and have always had great memories; and now I am discovering that it was all wrong! I am still not sure as to how much these things hurt me or how much they hurt You, but I am willing to learn. Please reveal Your perfect truth to me. Let me see my sin for what it is and how it has stolen from me that I might confess it to You and move on and know Your beautiful forgiveness. In Jesus' holy name I pray, Amen."

My Journal
continuing the journey...

date _____

CHAPTER 4

WHAT IS PURITY AND WHY IS IT IMPORTANT?

For the past four years I have had the unique pleasure of serving middle school students in our church. Every year our youth pastor covers the topic of "sex" in a series of sermons comparing God's plan to the world's. He often challenges our students to practice purity. When we break into small groups, one of the first questions I ask my group of girls is, "What is purity?" The most common answer I have received to this question is not to have sex before marriage. This is only partly right. As I have already stated, sex before marriage is always wrong. However, when it comes to the subject of purity, there is so much more involved. Refraining from premarital sex is just the tip of the iceberg. So, I will ask you, too—what exactly is purity and why is it important?

Let us first look at the literal definition of the word. For this, I will use Webster's dictionary. It defines purity as *"freedom from adulterating matter; cleanness or clearness; freedom from evil or sin; innocence; chastity."*[8] Because chastity is mentioned in the definition, I feel it is important to define this word also. Chastity is *"virtuousness; sexual abstinence; celibacy; decency or modesty."*[9] Both of these words are associated with moral excellence and being undefiled. The word "pure" or some derivative is mentioned in the King James Version of the Bible over 150 times, and that number doesn't even count synonyms. Obviously, this is an important aspect of who God is and how He desires for us to live our lives. It is vital that we understand this virtue in order to experience boundless

---

[8] Victoria Neufeldt, editor in chief, *Webster's New World College Dictionary, Third Edition*, (Simon & Schuster, Inc. 1997), p. 1092
[9] Victoria Neufeldt, editor in chief, *Webster's New World College Dictionary, Third Edition*, (Simon & Schuster, Inc. 1997), p. 237

intimacy within marriage and with God. We have to get this right!

When I think of pure as an adjective, the first thing that comes to mind is pure love. I can honestly say my love for God is pure. If you have children, grandchildren, nieces, or nephews that are infants or toddlers, you may also think about how the love you have for them is pure. There is something amazingly perfect about holding an infant to your breast while he or she sleeps and listening to the gentle breathing and gazing upon the pouty lips and upturned nose. This type of love is not clouded with ulterior motives or selfishness. If you haven't read 1 Corinthians 13:4-8 in a while, do so now. Pure love is patient, kind, without jealousy, humble, without boasting, considerate, not easily angered, forgiving, truthful, protecting, trusting, and never failing. Did you notice that not one sexual reference is included in that description? In fact, you would not dare have a sensual thought about an infant or toddler! That would be perverted; it's absolutely unthinkable! How could there be anything pure about that? Ah, now we are getting somewhere. How is having a sexual thought synonymous with pure love? It's not.

Jesus taught in Matthew 5:27-30, that to even think about adultery was the same as committing the act. He said the same thing about murder. God's standard doesn't just require us to remain physically pure; it requires us to remain spiritually pure in our thinking. If you are not thinking about sex, it is a lot harder to act upon it. Consider this: you cannot put this book down and pick it up again without thinking about it first. Every action we take requires thought first. God created us, and consequently, He knows more on this subject than we could even begin to understand. We know the power of the mind can do some amazing things; but, on the other hand, it can also wreak havoc in a life. Thus, purity has to start in a place where no one else can see, a place where it is easy to hide our desires and dreams. We fantasize and never even realize how those dreams are slowly stealing something very precious from us. Many times our virginity is lost before we even crawl into bed (or the backseat) with someone.

I have spoken to more than one young lady who has truly believed that passionately kissing a young man with her body pressed against his was okay. After all, she was still physically pure, and never in a million years would she have sex without being married. When being presented with this idea, I have always asked the young woman, "What were you thinking about while you were passionately kissing? More importantly, do you really think that the young man you had your body pressed up against wasn't thinking about sex?" Even if she had not been thinking about anything more than kissing, I can guarantee you that any young man with an ounce of life in him isn't thinking during an episode like the one I just described, "Oh, what a nice girl! She has such a great personality. And she's so smart!" No, on the contrary; his mind is racing to a place that it really shouldn't be. Although the girl may be able to remain pure in her thinking, if her actions have caused the boy to lust after her and desire more, then both are breaking God's perfect law. How is that, you may wonder. Let's go to God's holy Word to discover the answer to that question.

Proverbs 6:25 instructs our young men to refrain from lusting in their hearts after "her beauty." Colossians 3:5 charges us to *"Put to death, therefore, whatever belongs to your earthly nature: sexual immorality, impurity, lust, evil desires and greed, which is idolatry."* Daydreaming about having sex with anyone before marriage is against God's will. There is no getting around it. Jesus was perfectly clear when He said it makes no difference whether you are thinking about it or engaging in it, it is immoral; it is not pure. Remember our explanation of pure love? Sensual desires are not part of that description. Okay, you may be beginning to see how lustful desires might be morally wrong according to God's Word. But what about the girl who was able to remain chaste in her thoughts, what has she done wrong?

In Romans 14, Paul wrote to the church in Rome about "disputable matters." There were new Christian converts in Rome who were uncertain about what the new covenant and the old covenant (the Mosaic Laws) entailed. They were confused about dietary matters. Some of these new believers truly believed that it was a sin to eat and drink certain things. There was also a group of Christians who were more established in their faith who believed that it was not a sin to eat and drink these same items. Paul's teaching was quite simple: *"make up your mind not to put any stumbling block or obstacle in your brother's way."*[10] We are not to do anything which will cause another believer to sin, whether we believe it is transgressing or not. If God takes such a stance on "disputable matters," how much more will He hold accountable those who cause a fellow believer to fall over a matter which is clearly a sin?

More often than not, young ladies cause males through their actions or dress to stumble and fall in the area of sexual sin, and most of the time those same

---

[10] Romans 14:13

young ladies are clueless that they have done anything wrong. Our culture is quite accepting of revealing clothing and sexually promiscuous behavior. We see young people embracing all the time, their bodies pressed together in full frontal hugs and we do not think twice about it. Can I just say after being the mother of two teenage boys with hormones surging through their bodies, that young men notice every curve of any young lady pressed up against them. They notice the cleavage and the bare midriffs and the short shorts. It arouses them. Knowing what we do about God's teaching on remaining pure in thought and not causing our fellow brothers and sisters in Christ to fall into sin, how can we continue to dress or act in such a way whether it is in fashion or not?

I am just as guilty as the next for causing men to sin. I have also been guilty of fantasizing about sexual encounters. I really believed that it was okay since I wasn't acting out on my dreams. Now I see how damaging this behavior was. Reality is never quite as great as the virtual reality we can create in our minds. Also, fantasy is impersonal and requires little to no giving on our parts. It is as far from an intimate encounter as one can get. It objectifies an act which was designed to bring unity. Then when we are finally in a loving relationship with a considerate spouse, we are disappointed that he or she is not living up to our expectations. We think to ourselves, "I am not getting what I need." Sex has turned into a source of entertainment. We look upon it with about as much compassion as we do a blockbuster movie.

Purity is not a physical condition.

I cannot stress this enough. Thinking about sex will hurt you as much as the act itself. Purity is not a physical condition; it is a state of mind that requires self-control and sacrifice. If purity is merely of the flesh, why would Paul instruct wives to be "self-controlled and pure" in Titus 2? Being a wife means you have engaged in sex. Therefore, he is not speaking about a bodily state when he gives the imperative to be pure. This is something we must understand if we are to grasp the magnitude of what God's standard means. Our lives are to be based on a principle that most of us don't even know how to define. And what about sacrifice? What do we need to give up in order to live pure lives? Control of our thoughts. This is where the battle should be fought and won.

If you look at most of the covenants that were made in the Old Testament, they required sacrifice to seal the deal. We must not forget the most important covenant ever to be made between God and man. It required the ultimate sacrifice of our pure Savior. Ask yourself this—what would it have meant had Jesus not been completely pure, not just in deed but in thought also? He had to be without blemish; it was the only way for us to be saved. Jesus came to earth and lived a sin-free life. He was the bodily representation of purity. How would you feel about our Savior if you thought that He had been sexually attracted to Mary Magdalene? Would you still look upon Him as the perfect sacrifice that we know Him to be? For some reason, that would just tarnish the image. That is why we become somewhat outraged when people make false accusations about Jesus having a child or having a sexual encounter with any of the women mentioned in the Bible. It doesn't fit the character of God.

It isn't easy to renew our minds and not give in to our passions. We are a self-indulgent culture that knows little to nothing about what it means to delay gratification and wait—to sacrifice the thrill of the moment. And even if we are able to control our actions, please do not ask us to change our way of thinking. That would be going too far! Nonetheless, to be pure requires complete control over not just what we do, but also what we think.

In order to affirm this, we need to hear it in as many ways as we can. Read Matthew 15:18-20. In this passage, Jesus had been approached by the Pharisees because the disciples had not washed their hands before eating, which was a Jewish tradition established by man not God. The Pharisees were concerned about the act making them unclean.

Matthew 15:18-20

[18] But the things that come out of the mouth come from the heart, and these make a man 'unclean.' [19] For out of the heart come evil thoughts, murder, adultery, sexual immorality, theft, false testimony, slander. [20] These are what make a man 'unclean'; but eating with unwashed hands does not make him 'unclean.'

What did Jesus say makes a man unclean?

᭥ _____

_____

_____

_____

Jesus realized so well that the heart is what defiles man, not necessarily his actions. Our thoughts can destroy us while we appear to the world to be clean. Now read 1 Samuel 16:1-7.

1 Samuel 16:1-7

[1] The Lord said to Samuel, "How long will you mourn for Saul, since I have rejected him as king over Israel? Fill your horn with oil and be on your way; I am sending you to Jesse of Bethlehem. I have chosen one of his sons to be king."

[2] But Samuel said, "How can I go? Saul will hear about it and kill me."

The Lord said, "Take a heifer with you and say, 'I have come to sacrifice to the Lord.' [3] Invite Jesse to the sacrifice, and I will show you what to do. You are to anoint for me the one I indicate."

[4] Samuel did what the Lord said. When he arrived at Bethlehem, the elders of the town trembled when they met him. They asked, "Do you come in peace?"

[5] Samuel replied, "Yes, in peace; I have come to sacrifice to the Lord. Consecrate yourselves and come to the sacrifice with me." Then he consecrated Jesse and his sons and invited them to the sacrifice.

[6] When they arrived, Samuel saw Eliab and thought, "Surely the Lord's anointed stands here before the Lord."

[7] But the LORD said to Samuel, "Do not consider his appearance or his height, for I have rejected him. The LORD does not look at the things man looks at. Man looks at the outward appearance, but the LORD looks at the heart."

WHAT IS PURITY AND WHY IS IT IMPORTANT?

According to this passage, what concerns God most, how we appear to man or what God sees in our hearts?

Read Ephesians 5:1-5.

Ephesians 5:1-5

[1] Be imitators of God, therefore, as dearly loved children [2] and live a life of love, just as Christ loved us and gave himself up for us as a fragrant offering and sacrifice to God.

[3] But among you there must not be even a hint of sexual immorality, or of any kind of impurity, or of greed, because these are improper for God's holy people. [4] Nor should there be obscenity, foolish talk or coarse joking, which are out of place, but rather thanksgiving. [5] For of this you can be sure: No immoral, impure or greedy person—such a man is an idolater—has any inheritance in the kingdom of Christ and of God.

Should there be even a trace of impurity among believers? What actions and thoughts could be included in a "hint of sexual immorality"?

Read Romans 8:5-8.

> **Romans 8:5-8**
>
> [5] Those who live according to the sinful nature have their minds set on what that nature desires; but those who live in accordance with the Spirit have their minds set on what the Spirit desires. [6] The mind of sinful man is death, but the mind controlled by the Spirit is life and peace. [7] The sinful mind is hostile to God; it does not submit to God's law, nor can it do so. [8] Those controlled by the sinful nature cannot please God.

How important is it to let our thoughts be controlled by the Holy Spirit? What will the mind controlled by sinful desires lead to?

_____

_____

_____

_____

_____

_____

_____

We must set our minds on the things that God desires rather than what we desire. Our desires will lead to dissatisfaction and death. As Christians, we should no longer be controlled by our sinful nature. We have God's Holy Spirit living within us to help us overcome sin and live a life of peace. We are instructed in God's Word to be transformed by the renewing of our minds and then we will know God's perfect will[11]

---
[11] Romans 12:2

We cannot live in perfect communion with God while letting our thoughts indulge in sexual sin. We cannot expect to experience sexual intimacy with our spouse if we continue to contaminate God's gifts with our selfish wants. It is time to purify our thoughts and realize that by changing the way we think, we will change our lives. We can experience intimacy the way God intended it once we allow God to renew our minds with His Holy Spirit.

"Father God, help me to view purity through Your eyes. Help me to see my sin clearly. Let me realize that being pure takes more than refraining from certain actions. I want to have thoughts that are pleasing to you and which will bring intimacy to my relationship with my spouse. Please help me to honor You and my spouse with pure thoughts. In Jesus' name, Amen."

CHAPTER 5

How the thief destroys

God had a plan for Abraham and Sarah. This plan included a promise that all nations would be blessed through Abraham and his seed. The plan was perfect, all except for one little detail—Abraham and Sarah didn't like the timing. They didn't want to wait any longer. Hadn't they waited long enough? I mean really, Abraham had received the revelation years before, and he wasn't getting any younger. Why wait? So, Sarah came up with what she thought would be a better plan, and Abraham was more than willing to comply. She would give Abraham her servant Hagar to be his wife and to bear him the long awaited child. It worked! Hagar bore Abraham a son, Ishmael. And that's when the trouble began—trouble that has continued to brew until this day between the Israelites (Isaac's descendants) and the Arabs (Ishmael's descendants).

That is what happens when man thinks his plan will succeed over God's. We get impatient; we hate waiting for the good things, for which we believe we are entitled. Why can't we indulge in the pleasures of life? Why would God create such pleasurable things if He didn't want us to enjoy them? That's not who God is. He wants us to have fun, doesn't He? Yes, He does. But He also knows that some things are worth waiting for, and those same things need to be sheltered in order to preserve their value. Sex is one of those things.

In our backyard we have fruit trees and grape vines. Waiting for the fruit to ripen on the branch or the vine is hard during the late days of summer and early days of fall. However, the tartness of a not quite ripe grape is usually enough to keep me from picking the fruit before its time. I cannot tell you how many times I have gazed longingly upon a plum-colored grape, bursting with juice and thought, "Now it's time," and picked it, only to spit it out in disgust because it just wasn't ready to be harvested. We manage to do the same thing with sex. There it is, hanging on the vine, just ready to be plucked off and enjoyed. Our greedy fingers grab hold of it, consume it, and then spew it onto the ground, ruining the sweetness of what we might have known had we only waited. We rob ourselves of the sweetness that comes from the rush of that first kiss or the nerve-tingling excitement of that first embrace. Physical intimacy before marriage deprives us of the ultimate pleasure of that first bite.

God wants us to enjoy the intimacies of sex within the protective walls of a covenant relationship. Instead, we have traded the perfect for the passing pleasure of the moment and are suffering the consequences. Sex binds people in a way that nothing else can, and it also has the power to break people when it is abused. That is why God is so clear about sexual immorality and marriage. There are no gray areas. This is not one of those "disputable" matters. God has a plan, and the purpose of that plan is to protect marriages and His covenant relationship with believers.

Many times throughout the Bible, the relationship between the church (believers) and Christ is compared to a marriage. Isaiah 62:5b says, *"as a bridegroom rejoices over his bride, so will your God rejoice over you."* In Matthew 25, Jesus told the parable of the ten virgins, comparing His return to the bridegroom. Again, in Mark 2, Jesus refers to Himself as the bridegroom, and one of the clearest descriptions of the church as the bride of Christ is given in Revelation 19.

Paul tells us in Ephesians 5:22-23, that the relationship between Christ and the church is a "profound mystery." However, through the covenant of marriage, we can begin to understand that union. Marriage teaches us how to love unconditionally and how to sacrifice self for the sake of another. It teaches us respect and commitment. Through marriage we can begin to understand true intimacy, an internal knowledge, a oneness that can only be experienced within the union of marriage. By understanding this bond, we can better appreciate the connection we have with Christ and how He sacrificed Himself to bring us into the beautiful relationship we have with our God. Jesus Christ was the unblemished sacrifice—the only offering pure enough to die in our place and cover us with His righteousness. The blood of the purest Lamb brought us into covenant relationship. He committed one hundred percent. We were His only love. He never courted any other. He waited until the perfect time, and then He gave all He had to give. That is to be our model of marriage.

Ask yourself this, what would Jesus' sacrifice upon the cross mean had He been defiled in any way? What if He had entered into the covenant relationship with a past full of lust-filled fantasies and sexual impurity? I am not saying that Jesus wasn't fully man. He was, and as a man, He was a sexual being. He appreciated a beautiful woman just as much as any man does. However, He never desired a woman in an unhealthy, ungodly fashion. He never lusted. If He had given in to any temptation, including impure thoughts, it would have disqualified Him to be the Messiah, the Lamb of God, the perfect sacrifice suitable to die in our place and cover our sins. Do you see how coming into a covenant relationship defiled can fracture a bond before it is even made?

Satan knows how damaging premarital sex and impurity in thought and action are, more so than we will ever know. He knows that if marriages lose their value, our relationship with God loses its value. He knows that if he can attack the first union established by God, all others will fall apart too, including the most important one we have—that with God. We no longer value purity, holiness, what it means to be consecrated for God's use; in fact, we really do not even know what these words mean anymore. They have been redefined and secularized. Even the word "marriage" has been reinterpreted by our society so many times that we are no longer clear as to what it stands for. And the attack continues to this day. Sexual impurity is Satan's ace in the hole. He understands what this means; he gets the significance. Why can't we?

Premarital sex and impure sexual desires cheapen sex inside of marriage. The beauty of what God has in store is stolen. God created sex and the way He planned it is far better than any cheap, X-rated film—better than even the most romantic movie Hollywood can imagine. It is more pleasurable than the lust-driven, heat-of-the-moment romps portrayed in every soap opera with the perfectly chiseled male and exquisitely beautiful, well-proportioned blonde. It is finer than the photo shopped, airbrushed images in a magazine. It is even more exciting than forbidden love because it is not associated with guilt. There is no bitter aftertaste that stays with you robbing you of the sweetness of true sexual pleasure that satisfies with tenderness rather than tension. That is how God designed it. Why are we letting our sex-saturated culture snatch this away from us with its cheap, counterfeit version? And we wonder why our marriages lack intimacy and are falling apart at record rates? We have bought into a terrible lie. The world's offering to engage in sexual sin has turned physical intimacy into a form of self-indulgent, pleasure seeking entertainment. The value of love-making has been lost.

The reason our marriages lack physical intimacy is because sex shouldn't be an act of self-gratification and intense passion the way it is portrayed on television and on the big screen. It should be a moment of considerate, tender love-making. There should only be two people involved and not a host of memories clouding the moment and stealing the heart. When you have had physical encounters with people other than your spouse, it can be difficult to keep your mind in the moment and not fantasize about what it was like when you were single and sex was thrilling. Love-making may not be "thrilling;" it may be quite comfortable. There should be a familiarity and ease about it. It has a different sort of "excitement"; an excitement that is healthy and causes our affections to grow stronger and more sensitive to the needs of our spouse. That is how God designed it. And there is something delightful about the lack of intensity.

While we are on the subject of "self-gratification," I want to speak very briefly about one of the major players that has distorted our thinking as to what intimacy is—pornography. This poison has taken sex out of the realm of being relational and has turned it into something God never intended it to be. And when I speak of "pornography" I am not just speaking of "Playboy" or "Hustler." Pornography exists in our advertising, on billboards, in television programming, and in movies. It is even on the Disney Channel, where we can find a twelve year old girl's sexuality starting to be exploited and manipulated. We fail to see that sexual images in all forms of media remove intimacy from sex. The word intimate should conjure up feelings of closeness, oneness, trust, and friendship without reservation. Pornography is detached and isolated sexual arousal. In its very nature, it is in complete opposition to physical intimacy.

We have taken something that God created to bring unity and familiarity unlike any other act and have turned it into a public spectacle that hurts and humiliates. God's precious gift to marriages has been tarnished in every way imaginable. We have picked the fruit before its time and have spewed it out onto the cold, hard ground where it lies rotting, spreading its bitterness throughout the land. We have come up with a better plan and are suffering the consequences. This thief has lived among us for so long that we no longer recognize it for what it truly is. We have welcomed it into our lives, nourished it with our thoughts, and now it has grown and matured into a terrible monster robbing our lives. It has stolen the one thing we should have cherished above all others, God's delightful plan for marriage—intimacy.

Sex is not intimacy.

Sex as defined by our culture has absolutely nothing to do with physical intimacy. We have been fed obscene propaganda for so long that we think that what we see and hear all around us is what we should expect in a healthy sex-life after we are married. Then we get married and at some point, we become very disappointed. This is not what we signed up for. After nearly 20 years of marriage, I can tell you that love-making does evolve. If we do not change our way of thinking and realize that what we have come to believe as acceptable behavior is not how God designed it, marriage will become something of the distant past that we merely read about in our history books.

It is no accident that God compares the relationship between Him and Israel and between Christ and the church to a marriage. This should be our definition of intimacy. This mystery, full of exciting potential and harmony, is waiting at our fingertips. God wants us to comprehend this union more than any other. Sacrificial love, respect, loyalty, and purity should define our marriages. We cannot let the world rob our lives of this priceless gift any longer. God's desire is to be in an intimate relationship with us. Do you understand the gravity of that? It is the most amazing, mind-blowing thing I have ever come to realize. No wonder Satan has worked so hard to destroy intimacy inside of marriages!

It took me a long time to come to terms with my past and how I had damaged my marriage before I even met my husband. I came into our union with a duffel bag full of sexual sin slung over my shoulder. "Okay, I'm ready; I hope you don't mind if I bring along a few extra guests into our marriage. They won't bother us for the most part. In fact, I hardly ever think about them. Only when the going gets tough, or perhaps when I am not enjoying our love-making as much as I thought I would. They will keep us from getting too close. That way, if things don't work out, I won't be as hurt. I will always have this bag full of memories to fall back on. Oh, I see you have a bag, too. Well…this will be interesting.

Actually, I'm not sure how I feel about *your* bag."

Many of you have done the same thing. You have this black suitcase that you carried to the altar with you and have been lugging around ever since. Either you have openly displayed it, or it was hidden under your bridal gown. Either way, it has been robbing you of the joy God has waiting for you. It has been standing in the way of your relationship with Christ. It is time to bring it out into the open, lay it down, open it up, and give it to God. It is not until we can confront the thief that we can begin to know healing. Open your eyes. I promise you, God can destroy the thief before it destroys even a second more of your life.

I believe that for many, this has been the most eye-opening chapter. I know it was for me. It was years of God's gentle teaching that brought me to the realization that His standard of purity is so much higher than what I had first realized. And then it took even longer to see how defiling God's standard is destroying our marriages. Before we look at other common issues that tend to take away intimacy from our marriages, it is important to read a few more passages on the subject of sexual immorality and what God's standard is. Please read Romans 1:29-31.

Romans 1:29-31

[29] They have become filled with every kind of wickedness, evil, greed and depravity. They are full of envy, murder, strife, deceit and malice. They are gossips, [30] slanderers, God-haters, insolent, arrogant and boastful; they invent ways of doing evil; they disobey their parents; [31] they are senseless, faithless, heartless, ruthless.

What types of sin is "sexual immorality listed with?

༄ _____

_____

_____

_____

_____

Those are some pretty serious offenses. Did you realize that sexual immorality was listed right along with murder? Now read 1 Corinthians 6:18.

1 Corinthians 6:18

¹⁸ Flee from sexual immorality. All other sins a man commits are outside his body, but he who sins sexually, sins against his own body.

What are we to do when it comes to sexual immorality and why?

🕮 _____

_____

_____

To flee from something means to not even give it a second thought. You can't mull it over in your mind and then decide to leave. That is not fleeing, and most of the time if you give something too much thought, you will not be so quick to walk away from it. Satan can always find a compelling reason for you to stay. Flee means run! Do not pass go, do not collect $200. Just leave.

Now I want us to look at Ezekiel 16. I realize this is a long chapter; however, there is so much to learn from it. In it, God speaks to Ezekiel concerning Jerusalem. He uses an allegory here, comparing Israel to an infant that God found, kicking and bloody, despised by all. God nourished her and she became beautiful, but instead of giving her loyalty to her Caretaker, she broke faithfulness to God and gave her gifts to others.

Read verse 25 again.

Ezekiel 16:25

²⁵ At the head of every street you built your lofty shrines and degraded your beauty, offering your body with increasing promiscuity to anyone who passed by.

What did offering herself over to others do to Jerusalem's beauty?

Read verse 15-16.

Ezekiel 16:15-16

¹⁵ But you trusted in your beauty and used your fame to become a prostitute. You lavished your favors on anyone who passed by and your beauty became his. ¹⁶ You took some of your garments to make gaudy high places, where you carried on your prostitution. Such things should not happen, nor should they ever occur.

What did Jerusalem place her trust in?

From this chapter in Ezekiel, we learn that Jerusalem had been given wonderful gifts. But instead of cherishing those gifts and using them the way God intended, she cheapened them by entering into relationships with counterfeit lovers. She gave herself away and degraded her beauty. In the process, she damaged her relationship with God.

We have done the same thing. We have accepted counterfeit lovers and have used our sexuality to sell anything and everything. We have used our physical beauty to manipulate and maneuver through life. We have cheapened one of the most exquisite gifts God has given us and in the process damaged our relationship with our Maker. It is time to stop believing the lies. Sexual sin destroys and until we realize this simple fact, the intimacy we crave will never be ours.

"Father God, I have bought into the lie for too long. I did not see how my sexual promiscuity or lusts had damaged my marriage before I even said 'I do.' I came into the covenant relationship blemished. I picked the fruit, I let it rot, and now I need you to forgive me and restore me. I want to know my spouse in the way You designed. I want to experience lovemaking instead of 'sex'. I want the memories to be gone. Forgive me for where I have been. Now, I need You to take me forward to where You want me to be. In Jesus' name, Amen."

My Journal
continuing the journey...

date _____

CHAPTER 6

AN UNFORGIVABLE OBSTACLE:

WHEN THE SIN IS NOT OUR OWN

Before I leave the subject of sexual immorality and how it creates an obstacle in our marriages, I need to address one more issue. Sometimes the decision to have sex before marriage is not our choice. What then? Are we doomed to never experience God's plan for our marriages? How do we move past something so horrendous?

This may be the most difficult and revealing chapter I have had to write and it may well be the most difficult chapter that you will ever have to read, but I know I am not alone in some of the horrors that I have experienced when it comes to sex. How one views sex before she enters into a marriage profoundly affects the intimacy she is able to enjoy with her husband. Before we can experience the abundant pleasures that God intends for us to experience in the marriage bed, we have to empty our closets of all the skeletons that lie hidden in the far corners among the cobwebs and piles of discarded clothing. This has not been easy for me. Not only am I cleaning out the closet, but I am also parading those hideous bones in the front yard for the entire world to see. However, if I did not display the carcasses that have littered my life and if I failed to reveal the deep wounds that have penetrated my heart, I could not speak to you of intimacy. For true intimacy is exposing the darkest moments and letting God's light illuminate the lessons that might be learned.

We had a dear, trusted friend of the family who was allowed to care for my sister and me whenever our mother went out with his wife. While he cared for us, often late into the night, he would send the rest of the children to bed and spend what he termed "special" time alone with me. I was eight, and although

I didn't understand completely what he was doing or how wrong it was, I knew it was painful and terribly frightening. I sobbed through this "special" time, calling pleadingly for my sister. Those pleas were often followed by a threat from my tormenter and were quite effective in silencing my cries. This was my first experience with sex.

Many years later, I found myself alone with an elderly, male family member. My mother had always warned me not to be alone with this man, but he was so kind and attentive I felt no danger. One day while returning some books he had allowed me to borrow, I quickly realized why I should have heeded those warnings. Suddenly, he pulled me onto his lap and made several sexual advances. Being a healthy eleven year old girl, I was able to struggle quite forcefully and free myself from his bony grasp. I ran as fast as my skinny little legs would take me to my mother and burst into tears. When I shared with her my tale of woe, she responded with exasperation and pain, "That's why I told you never to be alone with him!" And that was it, swept under the rug never to be mentioned again.

That's how sexual abuse was handled in the 70s. Everyone had an "uncle" or "grandpa" that required a special level of caution or complete avoidance. No one ever mentioned the reasons "why;" one was supposed to know without inquisition or explanation. This was quite convenient for the perpetrator, but beyond damaging for the victim. I'm quite convinced a generation of victims grew up never knowing how to deal with the mixed up emotions and detrimental effects the sexual abuse had on their sexual identity and intimacy in general.

Why, you may ask, have I opened the door of this long forgotten closet and spread out its contents for all to see? What does my past pain have to do with intimacy? Well, just about everything. Sexual abuse may arrest a woman's emotional development. It can prohibit the maturation of an individual's psychological growth, preventing intimate connections from ever being made in her life. If this type of abuse is never dealt with, the results can be horrendous. She may very well remain a target her entire life, never feeling as if she has the right to take control of her environment and disallow further exploitations. Fear of intimacy, resulting in a complete avoidance, may plague a victim's life. Other effects may be alcohol or substance abuse, eating disorders, depression, dysfunctional sexuality or a complete lack thereof. Women are unique in how they have been created; therefore, their coping mechanisms will also be unique. However, issues with intimacy tend to be the recurring theme in all who have been wounded by sexual abuse.

Another phenomenon among sufferers of sexual abuse is their tendency to become promiscuous, so much so that it is now considered one of the warning signs of sexual abuse. On the surface, it doesn't seem to make sense. Why would a woman engage in the very behavior that was utilized in her abuse? One reason may be that most victims involve themselves in self-destructive behaviors. There tends to be a lack of emotional attachment to the sexual act itself. Being exposed too early to sexual activity many times causes one to become hyper-sexualized—obsessed with the very behavior that caused his or her pain. It becomes a way of gaining attention or gaining control. Another underlying factor could be that sexual abuse robs its victim of self-esteem. When an individual's self-worth has been damaged, everything seems lost. What value does one have? The woman that has been sexually abused will many times view her sexuality as the only thing she has to offer and offer it freely to all who ask. With promiscuous behavior, once again, we see a dysfunctional view of intimacy, and, in most cases, the complete absence of it.

If you have been a casualty of sexual abuse and have never dealt with the effects of that abuse, I urge you now to seek Biblical counseling. Although God is the answer, this is one of those areas in your life where you truly need someone who specializes in counseling victims of abuse to guide you in the right direction and help you confront the issues at hand. You may find that certain emotions and fears that you could not explain may be the result of that abuse. Don't let this obstacle hinder you from becoming completely whole in the loving arms of Christ. He will give you healing and comfort that you never imagined possible. He will completely remove the road blocks that obstruct your path to complete intimacy with your spouse.

Even after years of counseling, I still struggle to maintain a healthy attitude in this area of my life. Old wounds open easily, and so many times I find myself nursing an injury unsure of its origin. I fail to see the connection between what happened all those years ago and how it may be connected to the here and now. The most important thing I have found is that I must maintain an open dialogue with my husband about how certain actions or words may trigger feelings of being victimized. When this occurs, I find myself shutting down emotionally or becoming angry and withdrawn. Communication is key. I cannot emphasize that enough.

Woody, even after all these years together and the effects of gravity, giving birth to and nursing three children, still finds me completely desirable and loves to express this in many ways. Any healthy, red-blooded American woman would love to have her husband's undivided attention and healthy showering of affections. Who wouldn't want to hear her husband exclaim, "You're hot!" when she walks into a room, or to have him stare at her longingly? A woman who has been sexually abused. I find myself hyper-sensitive to any word or deed that causes me to feel objectified and not wanting to be desired for my sexuality. I find myself becoming angry when my dear husband feels as if he's just paid me a compliment.

Although Woody has always been aware of my abuse, it wasn't until I began to write this chapter that he finally made the connection between some of my behaviors and the abuse that I had suffered. And this is where communication becomes so important. I need to relay to Woody what I'm feeling and why I'm feeling that way. Otherwise, he's blindsided by my resentment and bewildered as to what he did wrong. The last thing I want is for him to quit desiring me. He has a healthy, Biblical attitude towards the woman God has given him as his wife. If I cannot convey to him the depth of my emotions, how can I hope to obtain the emotional intimacy we need to have in order to experience the physical intimacy that God has created for marriage?

Again, I reiterate, if you have not dealt with such abuse in your life, get the help you need now. God has equipped certain individuals with the wisdom to assist others through this sort of thing. Until you have faced this crime down and have taken the necessary steps toward recovery, you will not experience absolute intimacy. You can know healing. God *desires* for you to be healed. Find restoration in His mighty, outstretched arms, the arms that were spread upon a cross to bear your sin and shame. He knows the pain of your heart. He has felt the pain of your heart. I stand before you as an example of the healing power of God guided by a Godly counselor. I have experienced restoration and know forgiveness. Do I still struggle on a daily basis? Yes, but with God's help I find the strength and wisdom necessary to overcome each and every day, and you will, too. Read Isaiah 40:29, 31.

AN UNFORGIVABLE OBSTACLE: WHEN THE SIN IS NOT OUR OWN

Isaiah 40:29

²⁹ He gives strength to the weary
and increases the power of the weak.

Isaiah 40:31

³¹ but those who hope in the Lord
will renew their strength.
They will soar on wings like eagles;
they will run and not grow weary,
they will walk and not be faint.

What does God give to the weary and weak?

_____

_____

_____

_____

_____

These verses tell us that God strengthens those who feel as if their strength is gone and empowers those who feel powerless. Can you imagine what it would be like to "soar on wings like eagles"? My oldest son is a budding ornithologist (someone who studies birds); therefore anytime I have a bird question, he is my "go to" man. Did you know the wingspan of some of the largest female bald eagles may be over 7.9 feet? The wingspan of a Golden eagle, which very well may have been the eagle Isaiah was referring to, can reach over 9 feet. Those are some powerful wings on a bird that is known for its strength and agility. I can just imagine sitting on the back of that majestic bird and soaring through the clouds, the wind whipping through my hair and feeling the dominance of such an amazing creature as it surveys the landscape with eyes that see even the tiniest movement. Now let's skip forward a chapter to Isaiah 41:10, 13.

Isaiah 41:10

¹⁰ So do not fear, for I am with you;

do not be dismayed, for I am your God.

I will strengthen you and help you;

I will uphold you with my righteous right hand.

Isaiah 41:13

¹³ For I am the Lord your God

who takes hold of your right hand

and says to you, Do not fear;

I will help you.

What command does God give us in these two verses?
I'll give you a hint, He says it three times.

 _____

_____

"Don't worry! Don't be afraid! Don't be dismayed" No matter what translation you read, the message is clear—do not fear! God promises to strengthen you, to take your hand, to uphold you, and to help you. He is the Lord your God! He has what it takes to hold you up and remove the things in your life that imprison you in fear. You are no longer a victim! Your God has stepped forward out of the dust that covers the battlefield and stands like a mighty pillar, the victor in your life. Let Him pick you up, dust you off, and give you back your ability to live an abundant life in His mighty arms!

*"My dear, Heavenly Father, I know You are
the God of all. I know Your power is infinite.
You alone can bring healing to my broken heart and
broken life. I have suffered at the hands of another,
but I know that Your loving hands are near,
ready to hold me and love me. Take away
the fear and shame. Give me a healthy view
of sexuality that I might enjoy the gift
You gave to be enjoyed in marriage.
In Jesus' name I pray, Amen"*

My Journal
continuing the journey...

date _____

CHAPTER 7

ANOTHER BARRIER

I hate it when God reveals something in my character that requires change, especially when I have become blind to the flaw and have been living comfortably with it for many years. However, after confronting my sexual sin I knew something was still blocking my way, preventing me from experiencing the intimacy with Woody for which I had been fervently praying. For years, I had been pleading that God would reveal what I could not see. Yet, when He made it perfectly transparent, I wanted to close my eyes and plead ignorance.

When I felt God's calling on my life to write a Bible study on restoring intimacy in a marriage, I was resistant. I was quite sure that God had called the wrong person. Most of my married life had been spent struggling with intimacy. Yes, God had brought Woody and me so far in our marriage, and I well understood how sexual impurity had damaged our bond. Nevertheless, I knew that we weren't where we needed to be quite yet. Something was still obstructing my view into God's perfect plan. I could not see what was in the way. "What is it?" I questioned over and over. "Why are you asking me to write about this when I still don't know all the answers? Not to mention I'm still wrestling with my heart."

Jeremiah 33:3 says *"Call to me and I will answer you and tell you great and unsearchable things you do not know."* That is exactly what I did. I went right to the source and begged for Him to show me what was still standing in the way of knowing my husband the way I longed to know him. Well, it was me. It was my fear and selfishness. It was my lack of ability to love completely and my desire to be alone. That was not the answer I was looking for.

This is hard for me to write but even harder for me to admit. The greatest barrier from my past that had prevented me from having complete intimacy with my husband was the fear of being hurt or the fear of loving. I had so many well-established defense mechanisms in place, that my heart had become nearly impenetrable. Although this fear was deeply rooted in my childhood, the long string of failed relationships and the sexual abuse I had experienced in my teen years and into my twenties had nourished this anxiety until it had become fully grown, preventing me from wholly loving anyone.

For so long and in so many ways, I have known abandonment, lack of intimacy, selfishness, and apathy. As a small child I was plagued by terrifying dreams in which I would find myself alone in our house. I would call out for my mother and father without any response. I *had been abandoned with no warning.* I would wake from these dreams trembling with fear and crying uncontrollably.

However, over the years, these dreams no longer frightened me. Somewhere along the way, I welcomed them like a long lost friend. I embraced the solitude. I yearned to be completely alone. I had built a wall around my heart and I would never be broken by someone's choice to not love me or to leave me. I would not be crushed by a world that so often felt as if it were closing in on me, devouring my innocence and robbing me of hope. I would survive! If that meant never letting anyone close enough to leave me vulnerable, then it was a small price to pay.

I have loved many people throughout the years, but only enough to give them security in our relationship. I always knew that if whomever I loved chose to end the relationship for any reason, I would be okay. I loved at arm's length.

Unfortunately, that habit was set by the time I met Woody and I wasn't about to change just because we were entering into marriage. After all, what if somewhere down the line he changed his mind and left? Or what if he had an affair? I had to come out on top. I could not be broken by the actions of another person. Even after becoming a Christian and knowing unconditional love, I still found myself pulling back. Something kept me from going the extra mile and truly loving completely.

When God created man, he immediately recognized that "*It is not good for the man to be alone. I will make a helper suitable for him."*[12] God knew this because He had created man with the desire to be with someone of the opposite sex. Although Adam had been in perfect communion with God, he had still longed for human companionship. After God created Eve, Adam's longing was completely satisfied. When I became a Christian, I was convinced that God would complete me, therefore, companionship was unnecessary. However, a longing for a relationship with the opposite sex was created in our being. It was not until after God created them male and female that He made the observation that all was perfect. It was not until the fall of man that this desire was distorted and morphed into something quite different than what God designed. Now, in our sinful state, that longing has been replaced or is nonexistent. I had been searching for fulfillment in God alone, not realizing He had designed me to find complete joy in my marriage.

This revelation opened my eyes to see what was preventing me from loving Woody entirely. I realized then that my fear needed to be eradicated in order to love Woody as God designed a woman to love her husband.

As I have mentioned before, it is so easy to know something in your head and be completely ignorant of it in your heart. I knew all the teachings on love. I knew all the teachings on marriage. "I love people," I would say to myself; and I truly did—as long as they didn't try to get too close. I loved without sacrifice. I loved selfishly. Unfortunately, I loved Woody the least of all. Don't get me wrong—I had a deep affection for him and loved him dearly as a friend (most of the time); however, when it came to giving of myself and turning to the needs of others, he was at the bottom of my increasingly long list. He was behind my children, my sister, my friends at church, my small group, even my pre-school students in Sunday school. Every time I took on a new ministry, his place on the list dropped. Plus, I haven't even begun to list my interests, because the truth of the matter was that he came behind all those things too.

Woody had repeatedly proven that he wasn't going anywhere. He had endured my selfishness and lack of interest for years with patience and love. He had done everything possible to earn my trust—to earn my love. What in the world was wrong with me? It took prayer and reflection to discover the problem. Every

---

[12] Genesis 2:18

time Woody had "failed" me, I had held on to my injury. I had nursed it and kept it alive until it completely took over and blinded me to all of my dear husband's wonderful assets.

I could no longer see the hard-working provider who sacrificially went to work every day to provide for his family. I could not see the help mate who would come home after a long day at the office and help me with dinner and dishes. I was blind to the man who would sit through his daughter's three hour dance recital or his son's four hour karate belt test. And I no longer heard the words of encouragement, the compliments, the terms of endearment, or saw the way he looked at me with love and admiration. I only heard the words spoken in anger or remembered the time he didn't help or in his humanness, unintentionally hurt me. Not once did I hold myself accountable for all the times I had wounded him. It was truly all about me.

My fear of being hurt was actually a cover for the self-absorbed world view I had come to believe in. That is what fear does; it places all the focus on self. So often we fail to see that our fear is essentially a focus issue. Trusting God with our lives and salvation means trusting Him with everything. That means He must become our focus. If fear is to be conquered, we have to change the way we view the world from self-centered to God-centered.

The first step in shaking this crippling thief from our lives is to call it by name. I had to admit to myself, and more importantly, to my husband, that I didn't love him completely. That is not an easy conversation to have! We are so good at hiding our true feelings. Our culture is full of superficiality, or should I say we are so "politically correct." Lies permeate our society—in advertising, in reporting, in politics. It is hard to sift through all the filth we are fed on a daily basis and discover the truth. From infancy on, we are encouraged to hide our true nature and to squeeze into a mold that may or may not fit who we are. We enter into marriage so often dreading the day our spouse will find out who we really are. Transparency? Honesty? Who speaks such nonsense? Yet, in order to experience emotional intimacy, we must speak truthfully. We have to take the mask off and say, "Here I am. This is what I really feel." Love must be without hypocrisy.[13] Once the thief is exposed, we can begin to battle against the lies.

---

[13] Romans 12:9

An inability to or fear of trust can be caused by many different factors. You may find that yours is rooted in abandonment or abuse. Whatever the cause there is only one cure. We must learn to trust in order to eradicate this poison from our lives. Learning to trust in God is an enormous feat for many. Every morning requires complete submission to an unseen Savior, and then trusting that same invisible God to manage your whole life. It is the craziest thing I have ever done! However, as you learn to trust in Him, your trust in human beings will also be restored. As the focus changes from your fear to your faith, relationships are rebuilt. Healing comes like a soothing balm. Man will always fail us, just as I will always fail others. However, believing in God to pick up the pieces and carry me through each and every storm allows me to trust and fully love. If the worst case scenario does come into play, God *will* be there. He will never leave my side. That reassurance gives me the courage to jump in with both feet without any apprehension that I might drown. I am being held by my Heavenly Father. What better life preserver could there be?

This is not easy nor does it happen overnight. It may take months of going through the motions and daily surrendering control back over to God. Remember, you are not placing your faith in human nature but in God. You are trusting Him to be who He says He is. You are believing in His promises. Once you do, it will allow you to trust your spouse and love him completely without the dread of being injured once again. I am not saying that your spouse will all of a sudden turn into a saint and never utter another word or repeat an action that causes you heartache. What I am saying is that God will always be there to comfort you and love you perfectly. He will be your solace. He will be your strong tower.

I believe that looking at God's promises and what He has to say about fear will help in exterminating this destructive force from our lives. Read Luke 12:4-7.

Luke 12:4-7

[4] "I tell you, my friends, do not be afraid of those who kill the body and after that can do no more. [5] But I will show you whom you should fear; Fear him who, after the killing of the body, has power to throw you into hell. Yes, I tell you, fear him. [6] Are not five sparrows sold for two pennies? Yet not one of them is forgotten by God. [7] Indeed, the very hairs of your head are all numbered. Don't be afraid; you are worth more than many sparrows.

According to this passage what should we fear? What should we not be afraid of? Who values your life more than you do?

૱ _____

_____

_____

_____

God knows the number of hairs on your head. He even keeps track of how many you lose every day. If something of so little value is counted by God, how much more will He care for your heart? Now go to Romans 12:9-21.

Romans 12:9-21

[9] Love must be sincere. Hate what is evil; cling to what is good. [10] Be devoted to one another in brotherly love. Honor one another above yourselves. [11] Never be lacking in zeal, but keep your spiritual fervor, serving the Lord. [12] Be joyful in hope, patient in affliction, faithful in prayer. [13] Share with God's people who are in need. Practice hospitality.

[14] Bless those who persecute you; bless and do not curse. [15] Rejoice with those who rejoice; mourn with those who mourn. [16] Live in harmony with one another. Do not be proud, but be willing to associate with people of low position. Do not be conceited.

[17] Do not repay anyone evil for evil. Be careful to do what is right in the eyes of everybody. [18] If it is possible, as far as it depends on you, live at peace with everyone. [19] Do not take revenge my friends, but leave room for God's wrath, for it is written: "It is mine to avenge; I will repay," says the Lord. [20] On the contrary:

"If your enemy is hungry, feed him;

if he is thirsty, give him something to drink.

In doing this, you will heap burning coals on his head."

[21] Do not be overcome by evil, but overcome evil with good.

When we love others, who are we serving? What about when we are mistreated? Is that an excuse to stop loving—to stop trusting? Who will avenge you?

Loving others is serving God, even when they mistreat us. God has our back. We do not need to worry about "karma." It is not our job to keep score. God is the perfect judge. We need not concern ourselves with justice. God has it handled.

I would like you to read Ephesians 5:1-2.

Ephesians 5:1-2

[1] Be imitators of God, therefore, as dearly loved children [2] and live a life of love, just as Christ loved us and gave himself up for us as a fragrant offering and sacrifice to God.

What did loving us cost Jesus Christ? How are we to live?

I want you to really think about this. Jesus Christ paid the ultimate price when it came to expressing His love for us. Were we worthy of His gift? Did we do anything in advance to deserve what He gave us when He gave up His life? Did we earn His trust? Can we be trusted even now to do the right thing? The answer is no to all of those questions. Thankfully, Jesus was not too worried about himself or the suffering He would endure; otherwise, He would not have followed through with His sacrificial death. His focus was on the world. He had far more to be anxious about than we will ever have to experience in our lives. Still, His faith was in the Father just as ours should be.

If worry of being hurt or abandoned has caused you to pull back from your spouse, it is time to face it head on. Talk to God and then, talk to your spouse. Let honesty break the chains that have held you to the ground and have kept you from soaring. After you have done that, a change of scenery is in order. No more looking at self and trusting in your own ability. If you are anything like me, your own attempts to preserve your heart from hurt have left you feeling empty and bruised. Trust God. Hand it over to Him. Once you do, He will guard what is His against all principalities. Only He has the power to do so.

"Father God, help me to face the truth of my fear. Help me to be honest with You and my spouse. I want to move forward. I want to remove this toxin from my life that I might now have true emotional intimacy with my love. Help me to put my faith in You—You can be trusted to hold me through every fall. You have my heart in Your very capable hands. Let me love sacrificially that I might finally realize the security You have waiting for me. In Jesus' holy name I pray, Amen."

My Journal
continuing the journey...

date _____

CHAPTER 8

Now what?

David had it all. He was king over one of the most powerful nations. He had fame and fortune. He had a beautiful family with several beautiful women who called him "master." Most importantly, he had found favor in God's eyes. Yet one balmy spring night when he should have been out in the trenches fighting with his men, he grew restless. He paced the roof of his palace. He was bored. And then he saw her! There on a nearby rooftop, a gorgeous dark-eyed beauty with bronze skin and long flowing hair bathed in the moonlight. "That's what I'm missing!" Quickly he sent for a servant. "Go! Find out all you can about that woman."

The servant took one look at the woman and recognition filled his eyes. Hesitantly, he tried to send a subtle warning to the king. "Isn't that Bathsheba? Isn't she married to Uriah?" David ignored the warning and sent his servants to fetch her. They brought her to the palace and David spent the evening with her. We don't have to ask what they were doing because we learn from 2 Samuel 11, that she had just finished purifying herself from her menstrual cycle. Then, lo and behold, we read that Bathsheba is sending word to David to inform him of her pregnancy.

Most people are familiar with this story and know that in order to hide his sin (and to avoid being killed, which was the penalty for adultery), David had Uriah killed. When the time of mourning was over for Bathsheba, David brought her to the palace to be his wife. She gave birth to a son, and for a while they were a happy little family. What most people fail to see in this story is that for nearly a year, maybe even longer, David and Bathsheba lived hiding their sin, appearing quite content. Nothing seemed to change. In fact, Bathsheba's situation had greatly improved. David still had his power and his fortune. They were prepared for "happily ever after." David seemed to be completely oblivious to the sins he had committed.

Isn't that just like us? We do things that are against God's plan for us—against His precepts—but the things we do are so common in our society that we fail to see the error in our actions. We cover up our sins so well from other Christians, and we live as if it never happened. Our sexual sins and our impurities get buried in the backyard, and we try our darndest to completely forget. We never deal with our sins.

David didn't deal with his sin until Nathan the prophet came to him with the story about the two lambs. David was furious over the injustice and still failed to recognize his own sin. Not until Nathan said, "You are the man," and proceeded to proclaim what the consequences of that sin would be did David identify himself as the offender. What did David do then? Did he make excuses or try to hide what he had done? No. Instead, David quickly confessed his sin, acknowledged his guilt, and took responsibility for his actions. His confession was heartfelt, and though he pleaded with God to spare the life of his son, when the child died, David still worshiped God.

Perhaps you are coming to terms with your past for the first time, or perhaps you have faced it down before but were completely unaware of just how damaging sexual sin is to a marriage. Whatever the case may be, the first step in moving towards restoration is acknowledging our sin and confessing it. We cannot move towards God's beautiful forgiveness and grace until we have truly mourned for our sin and taken complete responsibility for it.

What is our greatest need?

Forgiveness is our greatest need. We are just like the paralytic man in Mark 2. I am sure that at first it must have seemed as if Jesus had completely bypassed the poor invalid's utmost need. However, Jesus knows that we need forgiveness before we can be healed. Do you realize this? You must seek His mercy before the healing can come. Do you crave healing for your marriage so much so that you are willing to break through a ceiling to receive it? If so, you must understand that until we have acknowledged our sins, healing will not occur. I knew that until I mourned for each and every person I had harmed through my actions, I could not move towards God's promise to rebuild my marriage. Every person, every faceless stranger in my past whom I knew my actions had wounded I had to lift up before my holy God and say, "I am so sorry! This was so wrong! Please forgive me."

Once we have confessed our sin, we need to acknowledge our guilt and take responsibility for our actions. That's where it might get a little tough. Part of taking responsibility for our past transgression is making apologies to all parties involved. David didn't have to just apologize to God. He also had to apologize to Bathsheba. We read in chapter twelve verse 24, that David went to Bathsheba and comforted her. I am sure that part of that solace included a sincere apology for violating her and in turn causing her even more pain with the loss of their son. So, to whom do you need to apologize? For starters, your spouse. He doesn't need to hear all the gory details, but he does need to know that you were sexually impure and that you regret those actions or thoughts. If he has a past, this would be a good time for him to make his apologies too. Ask for forgiveness for cheating each other out of God's perfect plan. Promise to lay down the thoughts that were coming between you.

Next comes what I believe to be the most humbling part of this process. Ask God to whom from your past you owe an apology. I do not recommend that this be done face to face. After much prayer you may write a letter or compose an email. Keep it short and to the point. It can be as simple as, "I want to apologize to you for our past relationship. I now realize that it was immoral and damaging. Although what happened between us was years ago and we have both moved on, I cannot move forward in my spiritual journey until I take responsibility for my sin. I did not remain pure as was God's plan for us both. Please forgive me." You may not be able to deliver your letter; but just the act of writing it and admitting to yourself that, yes, this was wrong helps in putting it behind you. Too many times when dealing with past "loves" we have a tendency to romanticize the times gone by. "We had some great times," might be your reaction when seeing someone from your past. Penning your confession closes the door on those reminiscences. We have to view our sin for what it was—wickedness done before a holy God—and then mourn for our actions. When you can admit that your behavior was against God's will, you can then shut the door and say "No!" with conviction when the memories start to creep up on you.

I have done this. I have sent a few emails or messages on social media and never heard another word. I am sure I must have appeared to have gone mad. But I am so grateful that I did. It really did close a door that I had left open just a crack. Now that door is bolted shut. We cannot hold on to anyone from our past if we hope to live intimately with our spouse in the present. It is not possible. You might as well pull up a chair beside your bed and say, "Oh, I hope you don't mind that I brought John into the bedroom with us tonight. That's not a problem, is it?" Do not let pride stand in the way of your freedom. Having one more person in this world who thinks I am one of those "crazy Christians" is okay by me. So I might have lost the good opinion of someone who was once important to me, but what I have gained is so much better.

Complete confession is complete surrender. It means turning away from your sin. We can't keep looking back over our shoulder wondering what might have been. I know it is not easy writing about your past mistakes. This whole book has been that for me. Here it is! My scandalous history in black and white for the entire world to see including my children who, up to this point, have likened me to Mother Teresa in matters of sexual morality. However, in order to be free and to help someone else discover the same liberty, I would write about these things a million times more.

If you find yourself unable to admit in written word that your past behavior or your lust was wrong, you may never be able to make it over this wall. God is waiting to pick you up and carry you over to the other side, but you have to confess first. In order to know complete intimacy we must first come face to face with our sin and admit it was exactly that—sin! Then, and only then, can we start moving toward God's miraculous rebuilding of our marriages.

If we continue the story of David in 2 Samuel 12, we find that after his confession and acknowledgment of guilt, David was restored to an intimate relationship with God; and in turn his relationship was also restored with Bathsheba. We know this because God gave them Solomon, and verses 24 and 25 tell us that God loved Solomon and sent word to Nathan to rename Solomon Jedidiah which means, "Darling of Jehovah."[14] God blessed their marriage even though they had

---

[14] William Smith, LL.D., *Smith's Bible Dictionary* (Spire Books, 1984), p. 269

completely defiled the marriage bed. Why? Because they repented and turned away from their sin. God is waiting to do the same thing for your marriage.

Before we discover how God redeems our marriages, let us take a look at David's story and his admission of guilt.

Read 2 Samuel 12.

What does David say once he realizes his sin? What reassurance does Nathan give him concerning his sin?

David admits to his sin, but Nathan assures him that God has removed his sin, just like that. The admission was made and forgiveness was given. There were still consequences to be paid.

What were some of the consequences?

Our sexual sin may not seem to have as dire consequences as David's did, but if you really consider what is at stake—the death of intimacy—we are suffering just as he did. Also, did you see what Nathan told David in verse 11? *"Out of your own household I am going to bring calamity upon you."* Isn't that what we are experiencing? I know that for fifteen years I suffered that calamity before I finally fell to my knees and dealt with my sexual sin. And although God has removed my sin, I am still suffering the consequences of what I did all those years ago.

Now let us read David's prayer for forgiveness in Psalm 51. This was written after Nathan confronted David with his sin. Read the whole psalm.

How sincere does David sound? What sacrifices does God want from us?

_____

_____

_____

I love the poetic language of this psalm. David's pain is audible. He knows that God alone can restore joy and cleanse him from his iniquity. He also knows that his life is worthless if he cannot approach God with a broken and contrite heart. He must be remorseful.

I would like us to look at one more psalm written by David, Psalm 32.

How did David's sin make him feel when he denied it? Contrast those feelings with how he felt once he admitted to it.

_____

_____

_____

We are not sure of what incident David is speaking. What we can be sure of is how he felt when he refused to acknowledge his sin and attempted to run from it. His strength was gone; his bones wasted away. However, once he acknowledged and confessed his sin, God forgave him and removed the guilt of that sin. He was able to rejoice and affirm that "Blessed is he whose transgressions are forgiven!"

Your guilt does not have to weigh you down and sap the life from your marriage one day longer. You can fall to your knees right now and have your sins covered. God is waiting to remove that duffel bag of regrets slung over your shoulder. Let him lift you up over the wall. You will love what is waiting for you on the other side.

"Father God, I really need help with this.
How do I put down something that I have carried
for so long? Please take this from me.
Help me face my sin and take responsibility for it.
Help me to apologize to my spouse for what
I have cheated him of. Reveal to me whom
else I need to apologize to. I want to close the door
on all those memories so that I might make
new and better ones with my spouse.
In Jesus' name, Amen."

My Journal
continuing the journey...

date _____

CHAPTER 9

MAKING ALL THINGS NEW

As a visual artist I love to create, and one of the most enjoyable mediums I have ever had the pleasure of working with is clay, more specifically, a pottery wheel. I could sit for days, covered to my elbows with the slimy slip, throwing, centering, and forming—until a well-curved pot is formed. In my opinion, the most challenging skill to learn when working with a pottery wheel is how to center the clay. It takes stability and quite a bit of force. I set my right elbow into my thigh and use it as a guide as I use my left hand to press the clay down. After that, I use both hands, cup them around the clay and bring it up as I continue to center it. You know the clay is not centered when it wobbles uncontrollably. First I learned to center the clay, then I had to acquire the skill needed to shape the clay into something useful, a vessel of some sort. It is not as easy as a talented potter makes it look. I cannot tell you how many times I have manipulated the clay into a bowl or vase only to discover that it was not centered or uneven and then had to start over.

Having worked with clay, I can better appreciate the comparison made in Jeremiah 18. God instructed Jeremiah to go to the potter's workshop. Jeremiah went and while he was there, he witnessed the potter working with a lump of clay. I am sure he watched as the potter threw the clay onto the wheel, centered it, and then began shaping it. He must have watched in fascination as the potter shaped a pot, found that it was marred, pushed the clay toward the center and reshaped it into a new pot that he liked even better. The lesson in this for Jeremiah was that Israel was like the lump of clay; and God is the potter who can create something beautiful and useful from a cold, useless lump of clay, even when the clay is full of impurities and rebelliousness. God alone builds and tears down nations and individuals. In verses seven and eight, God tells Jeremiah, *"If at any time I announce that a nation or kingdom is to be uprooted, torn down and destroyed, and if that nation*

I warned repents of its evil, then I will relent and not inflict on it the disaster I had planned." When we repent, just as the clay in the potter's hands was remade, we are remade in God's hands. He can take your marred marriage and transform it into something lovely and valuable.

This may not always be easy. Centering the clay takes force and is not for the weak at heart. It is messy. Being pressed down and reshaped is often painful. When I finally came to the point of realizing that my past was affecting my present state of affairs, I had a hard time believing that God could repair all the damage I had done. I was positive that I had gone too far and that Woody and I were so detached that there was no way I could feel any type of intimacy with him. "I know you have forgiven me, Lord, but I really do not know how You are ever going to fix this mess. This isn't just a marred jug we're talking about. Our marriage is more like a cold piece of clay that isn't even centered on the potter's wheel yet. I'm up to my elbows in mud and haven't even begun to make any progress." I knew I could not do anything. But God is faithful. I have a whole book that speaks of His faithfulness, and from that holy book I have learned He can make all things new. Not to say it didn't include some uncomfortable adjustments on my part. Change is never easy, especially when it involves admitting you are in the wrong. Nonetheless, the results are well worth the discomfort.

Israel was chosen by God. He wooed her and protected her. He drew her into an intimate relationship with Him. However, Israel was unfaithful. If you read all of Jeremiah, you will see how God compared Israel to a prostitute and a donkey in heat. She was faithless in all she did, committing adultery with other gods and people. Israel did wicked things of which God did not approve, things that at the time were accepted and popular in the society they were living in. Through Jeremiah, God told Israel that He would make her a desolate place. However, at the same time God promised hope. He would raise up a righteous branch from the house of David. He would restore the marriage relationship between Himself and His chosen people. In Jeremiah 30 and 31, we read how God would ransom His bride and show her His compassion.

Hosea is another book in the Bible that speaks of Israel's adultery and God's restoration. Hosea was told to marry Gomer, an adulterous woman. He and Gomer had a child. Gomer gave birth to two more children, but from the meanings of their names, we can assume that these two were not Hosea's children. Gomer left

Hosea and, through a series of events we are not made privy to, became a slave. Hosea was told to go redeem Gomer and to love her. He paid for her with silver and barley, and then told her, "*You are to live with me…you are not to be intimate with any other man, and I will live with you.*"[15] This portrayal is a revealing look at how God would pursue his adulterous bride and then redeem her. Israel did go through a period of exile, but God still loved her and desired to take her back.

Why do I speak of Israel and God? Because our marriages have experienced some of the same events. The intimacy between God and Israel had been defiled by previous lovers; but when Israel confessed, she was restored, and we will be too. God takes our desolate places and transforms them into fertile grounds overflowing with milk and honey. What He did for Israel, He can do for our marriages. I truly believed that my situation was hopeless. In my own effort it absolutely was. Yet, when I took my brokenness to God, and pleaded, "Please repair the damage I have done," He gently led me on the path toward healing.

I have found so much comfort in reading the story of Israel's unfaithfulness and God's pursuit of them. I knew from reading His Word that God's desire is for our marriages to be fruitful in every way. He longs for us to know true intimacy. He is the author of love and the Creator of marriage. If anyone can repair our shattered relationships, it is He.

I had been just like Israel. In Jeremiah 16, God informs Israel of her wickedness, how she had turned away from Him in her stubbornness to follow her own heart. I had done the same. I had followed the world and listened to the advice of fools. I had been left to my own demise. Still, God loved me and continued to court me just as He did Israel. In Jeremiah 33:11, God promised to restore the fortunes of the land to Israel. They would be returned to their original state. There would be the voices of joy and gladness ringing through the air. I realized that what I needed in my marriage was supernatural intervention. I needed God to rebuild my marriage and take it to a place it had never been—the original state of marriage when God established it in the Garden of Eden.

Do you believe God can renew your marriage? Perhaps you suppose as I did that you have done too much. I do not know your story, but I know mine. I had resigned myself to accepting that I would never have the closeness with Woody

---

[15] Hosea 3:3

that I so desperately needed. I was sure that I would go to my grave having never known the full pleasures of marriage. I had convinced myself that it was "okay" because I had no one to blame except myself. I was suffering the consequences of my sin. I was carrying my guilt around with me, trying to hide it from view by smiling through my sorrow. Imagine my delight when through the story of Israel God revealed to me that I did not have to carry around my guilt one moment longer. Job 14:16-17 clearly states that God will not keep track of my sin and that my offenses will be sealed up in a bag and covered by Him. He has forgotten my past. I am the only one who digs it up, throws myself into the hole, and plays in the mud. I need to learn to stay out of the dirt and leave the past behind me.

I love Isaiah 62. The portrayal of God's love for His children is so perfect. He tells Israel that she will be called by a new name. She will be a "crown of splendor" and no longer deserted. She will be called "Hephzibah" and her land "Beulah" (literally "my delight is in her" and "married"[16]). God can breathe new life into a desolate place. He can bring the "delight" back into the desert. Do you get that? Your marriage can go from forsaken to delightful. Nothing is too far out of God's reach to be rescued!

In Jeremiah 3, God says to Israel, *"Return to me; I am merciful and I will not remain angry forever. Acknowledge your iniquity, return to me, and I will give you those who will feed you with knowledge and understanding."* God says the same thing to you. He stands with outstretched arms calling, "Return to Me, and I will bring you Zion." He yearns for your restoration more than you do.

Believing that God wants to reconcile our marriages is challenging. When I first came to this realization, it was a daily struggle. Every morning I would fall to my knees and ask for God to give me faith, to show me that He really was present in the middle of my predicament. I had to renew my thinking every day, sometimes several times a day. But I knew God's Word. I knew the story of Israel. I knew the story of every believer who has been made new through the redemptive blood of Christ. With that faith, I prayed and trusted that God would be faithful and mend my marriage. Truly, the first step in healing is believing.

While reading my morning devotion today, I was struck by Hannah's story of

---

[16] Isaiah 62:4, text notes; *The NIV Study Bible, 10th Anniversary Edition*, (The Zondervan Corporation, 1995), p. 1100

prayer for Samuel in 1 Samuel 1, in a way that I had never before been affected. While Hannah prayed for a child, she was completely depressed. Yet, she poured her heart out to God. Her slumped shoulders and red-rimmed eyes revealed the hopelessness she felt when Eli spotted her praying inside the temple. Then Eli said to her, "*May* God grant you what you have asked." He didn't say, "He *will.*" *May* is not a promise; it is a possibility. However, at just the suggestion that God would help her in her plight, Hannah immediately brightened. She went and ate and her face was no longer downcast. She was full of hope and joy. And that was merely at the idea that her desire might be fulfilled. What faith!

The thing is, God making all things new in your life is not just a suggestion. It is a promise! Yet, we lack the faith to imagine that God will do what He has said He will do. In Isaiah 43:25, He makes it clear to us that our sins are gone. *"I, even I, am he who blots out your transgressions, for my own sake, and remembers your sins no more."* God is still asking us today, "Can I not do with you as this potter?" The problem is not in the vow; it is in our ability to believe. If we could only be more like Hannah and know that God wants this for our marriages more than we do. If only we could have the confidence that He really does make all things new, we would pray for it and live with hopeful expectation.

It is not easy. I have been on my knees too many times to count praying for the same renewal. I am here to tell you, God does answer prayer. The fact that my marriage has been made new is a testament to God's great power and grace. When I first began this journey, Woody was still spiritually immature without any desire to grow. I don't even think he was aware that our marriage was in trouble. He knew I was unhappy and that we didn't have a lot of emotional and spiritual intimacy, but he accepted it, never even realizing how wonderful it could be. God changed all that!

We serve a gracious, loving God. He can and will take your marred marriage and reshape it into something delightful. Believing is only the first step. Before we investigate the next steps, let us spend some time meditating on what God's Word says about restoring relationships and breathing new life into our desolate places.

Let us start in 2 Kings 18 and 19. King Hezekiah of Jerusalem was being threatened by the king of Assyria. It appeared as if there was no chance for Judah, yet even in the face of an enemy which threatened to wipe out this small nation, Hezekiah went into the temple of God and spread his worries out before the Lord.

Read Hezekiah's prayer in 2 Kings 19:14-19.

> **2 Kings 19:14-19**
>
> [14] Hezekiah received the letter from the messengers and read it. Then he went up to the temple of the Lord and spread it out before the Lord. [15] And Hezekiah prayed to the Lord: "O Lord, God of Israel, enthroned between the cherubim, you alone are God over all the kingdoms of the earth. You have made heaven and earth. [16] Give ear, O Lord, and hear; open your eyes, O Lord, and see; listen to the words Sennacherib has sent to insult the living God.
>
> [17] It is true, O Lord, that the Assyrian kings have laid waste these nations and their lands. [18] They have thrown their gods into the fire and destroyed them, for they were not gods but only wood and stone, fashioned by men's hands. [19] Now, O Lord our God, deliver us from his hand, so that all the kingdoms on earth may know that you alone, O lord, are God.

How did Hezekiah view the failures of the nations surrounding Jerusalem?

✍ _____

_____

_____

_____

Hezekiah knew nations had fallen to the king of Assyria. But he also knew that those same nations had not had the Lord God as their deliverer. Jerusalem was delivered and restored by the same God who promises to remove obstacles from your path and make your way straight. You may see marriages in ruins around you and feel hopeless in the face of such devastation. The power that saved the nation of Israel is accessible to you. When was the last time you spread your worries on the floor before the Lord and prayed with confidence for His deliverance?

Perhaps you have prayed with confidence for God's deliverance, yet you are still plagued with guilt. Read Zephaniah 3:15-17.

Zephaniah 3:15-17

¹⁵ The Lord has taken away your punishment,

    he has turned back your enemy.

The Lord, the King of Israel, is with you;

    never again will you fear any harm.

¹⁶ On that day

    they will say to Jerusalem,

Do not fear, O Zion;

    do not let your hands hang limp.

¹⁷ The Lord your God is with you,

    he is mighty to save

He will take great delight in you;

    he will quiet you with his love,

    he will rejoice over you with singing.

What does this passage say God has done with our punishment? Where is God?

_____

_____

_____

_____

Do you believe that God has taken your punishment and stands in the midst of your marriage? Perhaps you have never asked God to stand in the middle of your marriage and save the bonds of intimacy that should bind you together. The Mighty One stands ready to quiet your anxious heart and rejoice over you with singing. Have you ever thought about that?

No matter how desperate things may seem, nothing is too hard for God.

Read Habakkuk 3:17-19.

> **Habakkuk 3:17-19**
>
> ¹⁷ Though the fig tree does not bud
> and there are no grapes on the vines,
> though the olive crop fails
> and the fields produce no food,
> though there are no sheep in the pen
> and no cattle in the stalls,
> ¹⁸ yet I will rejoice in the Lord,
> I will be joyful in God my Savior.
> ¹⁹ The Sovereign Lord is my strength;
> he makes my feet like the feet of a deer,
> he enables me to go on the heights.

Do the circumstances described in verse 17 seem pretty dire? Nonetheless, where does Habakkuk find hope?

_____

_____

_____

Your marriage may not be producing any fruit at the moment, and you may believe you are walking in a barren land. Yet, just as the prophet Habakkuk rejoiced in the Lord, you too can rely on God to be your strength and know He will take you to new heights as He brings intimacy back into your relationship.

Before we leave this topic, I want you to read Isaiah 57:15-19.

Isaiah 57:15-19

¹⁵ For this is what the high and lofty One says—

    he who lives forever, whose name is holy:

"I live in a high and holy place,

    but also with him who is contrite and lowly in spirit,

to revive the spirit of the lowly

    and to revive the heart of the contrite.

¹⁶ I will not accuse forever,

    nor will I always be angry,

for then the spirit of man would grow faint before me—

    the breath of man that I have created.

¹⁷ I was enraged by his sinful greed;

    I punished him, and hid my face in anger,

    yet he kept on in his willful ways.

¹⁸ I have seen his ways, but I will heal him;

    I will guide him and restore comfort to him,

¹⁹   creating praise on the lips of the mourners in Israel.

Peace, peace, to those far and near,"

    says the Lord. "And I will heal them."

What things does God promise to do? What will He create?

_____

_____

_____

_____

_____

God tells us he will revive, heal, guide, and restore. He will create praise on our lips and give peace. God is nearby and with you ready to revive your marriage. He is prepared to restore intimacy. Only He has the power to do so.

Perhaps you are thinking as I did, "Great! I know God can restore intimacy; but what if we have never had intimacy? What then? Something that has never existed can't be renewed." Are you aware of what it means to create? Create means to make something new from what now is or to bring into being *something* from *nothing*. Only God has that kind of power. It is time to let go of your doubt. The God Who created the universe is the same God Who stands over your marriage able to fashion it into something amazing. Isn't it time to step forward in faith and know that you are on the road to restoration?

"Father God, only you can create something new from my brokenness. Only you can restore my marriage into something I was completely unaware it could be. Take away my fear and give me faith. Help me to come to You when I start to doubt and to never give up hope in what You are capable of. I know this may be a daily struggle, but daily You will be near my side, willing and able to make all things new. In Jesus' holy name I pray, Amen."

My Journal
continuing the journey...

date _____

CHAPTER 10

BUILDING ON SPIRITUAL INTIMACY

When I began on the journey towards intimacy, God led me to Exodus, chapter twenty-one. I had confronted my past with honesty and was looking forward to the present and future joy. I had identified the thief, understood what he had taken from me, confessed my sins, acknowledged my guilt, accepted God's forgiveness, and believed with all my heart that He could reinvent my marriage. So why was I still feeling a huge void? Woody and I had taken the correct steps, yet there was still this huge gulley between us, and no matter how desperately I tried, I could not see the way to the other side. "God, I need a bridge here," but nothing seemed to be falling miraculously from the sky. Then the light bulb moment finally came.

A few years ago while going through my beauty regiment, which may seem quite inadequate to most, I was pondering one thought—when would Woody lose interest in my physical attributes? I had just seen my 44th birthday come and go with very little fanfare. I was beginning to notice a few more fine lines travelling across my forehead and creeping down my neck. Although physically fit, there could very easily come a day when exercise no longer kept my abdominal wall flat and my arms firm. When would these tell-tale signs of age start to bother my adoring husband? That's when God spoke to me, quickly addressing my fears and giving me a solution for my aging body. Spiritual intimacy does not get old! It doesn't sag and develop laugh or frown lines. It doesn't turn gray or fall out. Spiritual intimacy grows more attractive as the years go by and develops into something so beautiful that all else pales in comparison. Had I been working on developing that kind of intimacy with Woody? Or had I spent more time focusing on the beauty that will always fade?

This was a huge wake up call for me. I was convicted on so many levels. I finally realized that the bridge I had been searching for was the same bridge that had connected me to God—Jesus Christ. He had to be the missing link. Without Him, we would never know complete emotional or physical intimacy. Spiritual intimacy is the foundation upon which all relationships have to be built in order to establish emotional intimacy.

It finally dawned on me that a basic need in my relationship with Woody was to be spiritually connected. I wanted to share my faith with him intimately. Yes, Woody was a believer, but he had not grown spiritually at the rate I had. I was leaps and bounds ahead of him, and at that point he showed no interest in catching up with me. I had asked him to do personal devotions with me. "No." I had mentioned group Bible studies. He would go to a few but never did the homework, and then he would become too busy with work and travel to attend anymore. We didn't pray together other than at meals. I couldn't even talk to him about my faith or God. I could converse for hours with my friends, but could only muster a few sentences when it came to talking with Woody. Why? With my friends I felt comfortable enough to talk about spiritual matters. We could talk about the glory of God and His work in our lives for days. I realized that Woody and I had grown apart because we were no longer interested in the same things. Unless it had to do with the kids or the house, we didn't talk. I didn't feel I could connect with him because I needed to be able to share the most important thing in my life, and if he wasn't interested, I didn't know what else to talk about. I needed more. If we were to grow emotionally in our relationship, we had to connect spiritually first.

Identifying the problem was a whole lot easier than trying to figure out what to do about it. I prayed. I asked God to change Woody's heart. I asked God to change my heart. Nothing seemed to work. Meanwhile, the gulf between us grew deeper and wider. "Are we even friends anymore?" I asked myself one morning. I didn't like the answer that seemed to stare me down and dare me to challenge it. Tears started flowing. For the first time in our relationship I was truly afraid that we had reached a hurdle that we could not jump over. What were my choices? I could either stay in a marriage in which I felt little to no spiritual connection, or I could leave and destroy the lives of five people in the process. I knew I would stay, but I was devastated at the thought that I would never know the joy I had so desperately sought since becoming a Christian—to share my love of Christ with my husband and to have him lead me into a deeper relationship with my Savior. I had given up.

My hope had vanished with every rejection I had received from Woody. I was afraid to ask again about devotions or praying together. Status quo would have to do.

And so life continued. From the outside looking in I am sure our lives seemed flawless. Our kids were flourishing, we never argued, and we were always doing things as a family. We attended church every week, where we both served in some capacity. What could possibly be wrong? Yet, I was growing increasingly frustrated and unhappy. "You never seem happy," Woody observed one morning. How could I tell him I wasn't? So, I told him he was imagining things, and life still continued to go on.

Who knows how long things may have continued in that holding pattern if God had not intervened. You see, throughout this period I had continued to pray and hold out hope that God was at work behind the scenes accomplishing what I could not. Although I had begun to believe that those prayers were bouncing around between the four walls in which they were uttered, they were being heard and attended to. One Sunday morning, after a heated Saturday night discussion in which Woody once again correctly accused me of never wanting to spend quality time with him, I was sitting at the kitchen table praying and reading my Bible when Woody called. He had gone to church that morning without me and was headed out of town on business. He had called to say goodbye. "I didn't realize you weren't coming home after church," I commented.

"I told you that last night. That's why I couldn't understand why you preferred to spend time with the kids or alone rather than me." His voice was still full of hurt and resentment. "What is wrong with you? You are never happy and you never want to spend any time with me."

I had been asking myself that same question all morning. What was wrong with me? I knew the answer but did not know how to tell Woody. "I am not having a basic need met," I finally managed to mumble. "I need spiritual intimacy. I need to pray with you and have a time of devotion. I need to be able to share intimately with you the most important thing in my life. If I can't, I'm not sure how much longer I can go on like this." Silence. "Do you understand what I'm saying?"

He finally responded, "I'm not sure I can give that to you."

"So, what are you saying? Are you even willing to try?"

"I'm not wired like that. It's just not for me." I was baffled by his reply. Was he saying what I thought he was saying? Was he willing to throw away over 15 years of marriage because he wasn't "wired" in such a way?

My mind was reeling. Fear grasped my heart once again. I finally managed to find my voice. "Are you willing to throw away all we have built over something like this?"

"I guess so if you don't think you can go on without it." At that point I hung up. Tears rolled down my cheeks. My heart was literally breaking.

"Lord," I sobbed, "You have to fix this. I am helpless. I can do nothing. Please! This can't be your will." I was sitting alone crying when I heard the garage door open. Woody walked into the kitchen. "I thought you weren't coming home," I remarked, puzzled by his presence.

"I wasn't. But I needed to get something." I started to go upstairs. I didn't want to face him at that moment. "Kim, wait! I came home to get the couples' devotion you bought and my Bible. I'm going to look it over while I'm gone; and if I don't like it, I'll go to the book store and find one that I do. I don't want to throw our marriage away. I love you too much!" At that point, we both were in tears. I fell into his arms, and we clung to each other realizing what we had almost lost.

That was the beginning of our marriage. Although Woody wasn't completely sold on the devotional I had purchased, he was willing to give it a try. "Be patient with me," he told me shortly thereafter. "I need to take baby steps."

The first morning we sat down together for a time of devotion was amazing. Woody read the passage. It was on the power of prayer and how prayer can determine the spiritual health of a marriage. Woody looked at me after the reading and asked, "What do you think about that?"

"It's so true. We do not pray together as we should. We need to be praying with and for each other." Woody took out his journal and a pen and asked me what he could be praying about for me that week. I then asked the same of him. After taking note of those things, we joined hands and prayed. He began, praying specifically for our marriage and my requests, and then I had the opportunity to lift up his needs to our mighty God. When we had finished, Woody's eyes were full of tears. It was an emotionally raw moment for us both because we had thrown off the masks and stood figuratively naked before each other. We were emotionally exposed. We had finally become one.

I cannot emphasize this point enough. Emotional and physical intimacy will completely break down if you are not spiritually intimate with your spouse. I have never loved my husband more than when he took my hands in his for the first time and prayed for me. Sharing our faith is building our marriage on the source of true love. Our shared faith binds us together in a way nothing else can. This is truly the starting point for every other type of intimacy. If you cannot share in this area, you are not being vulnerable to each other in the way we must be in order to experience authentic affection. There is a familiarity that comes through praying together and seeking God's will that you will find nowhere else.

If you are experiencing intimacy problems, I challenge you to examine your and your spouse's spiritual life. Do you pray together other than at meals and bedtime? Do you study God's Word together? Do you talk about how God is working in your lives? Do you worship together and praise God for whom He is?

I took a very informal survey when I was beginning this book asking Christian couples if they prayed together. I was surprised by the responses. The majority of couples do not. I then surveyed the couples who do pray together and asked them how praying together affected their emotional intimacy and their feelings of security. One of the responses I received impressed me enough to share with you. The following is an excerpt from this particular questionnaire.

> **"Does praying together give you a stronger sense of emotional intimacy?** Absolutely. It's a time when we can be truly raw and vulnerable together and feel completely safe. We often cry together during prayer and it is incomparable to any other intimacy I've ever experienced.
>
> **"Does praying together give you a sense of security? If not, why?** Without a doubt. Praying is our safe place. We come together before God and share our biggest fears. I know in those moments that my husband trusts no one the way that he trusts me, and my vulnerability gives him the same feeling."

If you are struggling in this area, a good place to start is prayer. You may think that you too need to take "baby steps" towards spiritual intimacy, and prayer is that first little step that needs to be taken on the path. It is as simple as making the decision to pray together instead of alone. There is no rule book here. Just make the time to join together and communicate with your Creator. It could take place standing in the kitchen in front of the coffee pot. You might look at your spouse, take his hand, and say, "Can we pray together for a minute?" It is very uncomplicated. You will be surprised at how quickly your relationship will grow once you have started. There will still be hurdles; Satan will give you every excuse not to pray. Children will cry, the phone will ring, work will press in, along with a million other things; but you will have to guard this time together like your lives depend upon it.

You may find yourself in a situation like I did, where your spouse refuses to grow in this area with you. Don't give up! If you get to the breaking point and feel as if you need more than prayer, seek Christian counseling. God will direct your path. Seek out people who will pray without ceasing for God to remove this road block from your marriage. I failed to do so, letting pride and shame keep me from one of the most powerful tools we have—intercessory prayer. I can't help but wonder if my failure to ask for help kept me buried in my grief longer than need be. Perhaps the timing would have been the same, but oh how comforting it would have been to have a friend to lift me and my situation up before the heavenly throne!

In Mark chapter 4:35-41, you can read one of my favorite stories of Jesus' miracles. The day was drawing to an end when Jesus and His disciples were in a boat in the Sea of Galilee. Jesus had instructed His disciples to cross over to the other side. The Sea of Galilee is surrounded by mountains and prone to violent storms. That day was no exception. Jesus had fallen asleep, exhausted from His teaching, when a furious storm threatened to overcome their meager vessel and drown them all in the process. The disciples fought in vain against the storm when someone finally decided perhaps it would be a good idea to wake up Jesus. At Jesus' command, the wind and the waves died down. As quickly as it had begun, it was over.

That is how I feel my battle for spiritual intimacy has been. I had brought Jesus along with me in the boat and was fruitlessly battling the storms in our marriage.

The torrential downpour had soaked us both to our feet, and I was beginning to feel as if we might sink when I finally cried out, "Teacher, do you not care that our marriage is perishing? Do you not care that we are about to drown?" At that point I had to decide what I believed in. Did I believe that Jesus had the power to stand up face to face with my storm and say, "Peace! Be still!" How often did He have to ask me, "Why are you so afraid? Do you *still* have no faith?"

You may be pleading now for God to bring your spouse around, to give him the desire to grow in this area. You may have given up. Whatever your situation you have to know that God does care! He can look at the vicious squalor that is threatening to pull you into the deepest trench and say, "Peace!" God's desire in your life is to discover an intimacy that surpasses all others. He can and will save you. David wrote, *"He reached down from on high and took hold on me; he drew me out of deep waters. He rescued me from my powerful enemy, from my foes, who were too strong for me."*[17] God is standing in the middle of your storm ready to draw you out of the deep waters and rescue you from the things which are too powerful for you to overcome. All you need do is believe.

Before we move on to emotional intimacy, I want us to explore a few stories and passages from the Bible which deal with this very topic. We are going to head back to Genesis 3, and Adam and Eve in the Garden of Eden. Read Genesis 3:1-13.

How did Adam and Eve feel after disobeying God's law?
What did they do when God went to the garden to seek them?

_____

_____

_____

_____

_____

---

[17] 2 Samuel 22:17-18

Read Genesis 2:25. This should be familiar. We read this same passage way back in chapter one. Adam and Eve were completely exposed and found comfort in each other. They were not ashamed nor did they try to hide from God or each other.

How does that feeling compare to their response in Genesis 3:7,10?

༄ _____

_____

_____

_____

_____

When Adam and Eve sinned they alienated themselves from God and each other. They attempted to hide, weaving together a covering of lies to conceal their nakedness. They immediately started shifting the blame. All of a sudden Adam no longer looked at Eve with awe and adoration as he had done when he first awoke to find his perfect gift from God. Instead he blamed her for his guilt. "It was this woman you gave me!" When man is estranged from God, every relationship he has will suffer.

Next is the story of David and his first wife, Michal. We are first introduced to Michal in 1 Samuel 18. She, the daughter of King Saul, was completely smitten by David, and for the price of two hundred Philistine foreskins, she became his wife. When Saul was trying to kill David, Michal helped David escape by taking an idol and laying it in their bed, covering it with a garment and goat's hair at the head and pretending that David was sick in bed. After that, David became a fugitive, Saul gave Michal to a man named Paltiel to be his wife, and we assume at that point that their great love story has ended. However, Michal comes back into play in 2 Samuel 3.

Read 1 Samuel 19:11-18; 2 Samuel 3:13-15; and 2 Samuel 6:12-23.

Does it strike you as odd that Michal had an idol in their home? Do you think this is an indication of Michal's spiritual beliefs? Also, what did she think of David's public display of worship towards God?

The fact that Michal had an idol in her and David's home speaks volumes about what she believed. Obviously, she and David were not on the same page spiritually speaking. Although they may have had a great relationship in the beginning (when the physical attraction was still strong), we can see that by 2 Samuel 6, the physical attraction was no longer binding the marriage. If you know the history of David and Michal's relationship, you know that Michal had many reasons which would have been motivation enough for her disgust with David. However, it was David's act of worship which pushed her over the edge. We have to wonder about the fact that Michal never had children. Could it be that she and David were never physically intimate again? I am not saying that is what happened, but the fact that Michal despised David and he was obviously not pleased with her could very well have led to a complete breakdown of physical intimacy. We know they did not share the same faith. We also know there were no emotional attachments between the two of them.

By that time, David had a few wives to choose from. It could very well be he chose to be physically comforted by one of his other wives who shared his faith. When faith cannot be shared, everything else will eventually fail. No matter how wonderfully it may have begun, the end will bring heartache and desolation.

Now we are going to read about another one of David's wives, Abigail. Abigail was married to Nabal, who literally was a fool. Read her story in 1 Samuel 25:1-44.

When Abigail discovered what her husband had done concerning David, how did she react? Did she treat Nabal with contempt? Even when she returned from seeing David, and she discovered Nabal drunk, did she confront her husband with his foolishness and lack of self-control?

_____

_____

_____

_____

_____

Abigail did not criticize or correct her husband. Instead she showed discernment and interceded with grace and kindness. There may have been many times when I thought Woody was a fool for not following God's perfect plan. However, like Abigail, I had to keep my mouth shut, intercede with prayer, and wait for the appropriate time to speak with grace and gentleness. Thankfully, things worked out better for Woody than they did for Nabal.

You may very well be waiting as Abigail did for the morning when you can speak to your spouse and say, "You are placing our marriage in harm's way. Everything we have is in danger of being lost!" Just know that God is not sleeping. He is at work moving the mountains, calming the storms. Trust in Him; He will not fail you. *"The LORD your God is with you, he is mighty to save. He will take great delight in you, he will quiet you with his love, he will rejoice over you with singing."*[18]

Just as God brought healing and spiritual intimacy to my marriage, He will do the same for you. For Jesus said, *"I tell you the truth, anyone who has faith in me will do what I have been doing. He will do even greater things than these, because I am going to the Father. And I will do whatever you ask in my name, so that the Son may bring glory to the Father. You may ask me for anything in my name, and I will do it."*[19] Will you start asking Him now?

"Lord, restore intimacy in my marriage. Open my spouse's heart and mind to Your love and wisdom. Give him the desire to pray with me and read from Your Word together. I believe there is power in Your Name—power to break down barriers and overcome that which I cannot. In Jesus' holy name I pray, Amen."

---

[18] Zephaniah 3:17
[19] John 14:12-14

My Journal

continuing the journey...

date _____

CHAPTER 11

An Emotional Bond

Friendship is one of the most valuable relationships in the world. We are told in God's Word that *"A friend loves at all times...."*[20] At *all* times? I have questioned that adjective more than once, and never have I questioned it more than in my marriage. The most difficult friendship to maintain is the one you have to face nearly twenty-four hours a day, seven days a week. But at the same time, it should be the most intimate friendship you have. It is rather impossible to not know someone intimately when you are waking up next to him with morning breath and surviving the time period between stepping out of bed and the first cup of coffee. Yet so many times the friendship in marriage seems to disappear. It gets buried in the day to day drudgery of work, carpools, children, and chores. You spend a lot of time talking to your spouse rather than with your spouse. Your conversations are filled with schedules and appointments that need to be met, discipline issues that necessitate action, and finances, finances, finances. There is no time to develop a fondness for the other's qualities or mind, and if you are not spiritually growing as a couple, there never will be. Then one day after ten plus years of marriage, children, and a mortgage, you may find you are sitting across the table from a stranger who occasionally provides physical comfort and shares in the family's responsibilities. Does this sound familiar? Perhaps, perhaps not; but that was my story. So much for loving at all times. Heck, I was struggling to like at any times.

As I have already mentioned in the previous chapter, I was sitting at that table, looking at a stranger, and wondering what I would do before God intervened and Woody and I began to develop spiritual intimacy. Praying together and spending time focusing on God's will in our lives was only the first step in rekindling our

---

[20] Proverbs 17:17a

fragmented friendship. Redeveloping damaged relationships of any sort requires time and diligence. Both parties have to be completely committed to rebuilding the friendship that first brought the two of them together. That is why it is so important that a couple start with developing spiritual intimacy. God will give both the desire to commit the time and work necessary to mend that which has been broken. And when I say time, I mean time! There is no short cut to contentment. Just as your marriage did not reach this place overnight, it will not be resolved within a twenty- four hour time frame. Perhaps you have heard the old proverb, "Good things come to those who wait." Do not give up while waiting. Be patient.

> *There is no short cut to contentment.*

I remember well the morning I awoke to discover that I loved Woody wholly. We had been praying together and completing morning devotions as much as our schedules would permit. During those times of prayer, there was something indescribable happening. A mutual respect and fondness was beginning to sprout. Throughout the day we started speaking more about each other—not the children, work, or finances. A friendship was starting to grow, ever so slowly. We were becoming reacquainted. Then one morning it hit me, "I love him, so much so that if I lost him, it would be devastating!" My heart had thawed, my walls had been demolished, and I realized I was with the man of which I had dreamed. The fear that had threatened to suffocate and the resentment that had developed from a lack of spiritual intimacy were gone. We were becoming best friends again.

A common misconception concerning friendship needs to be dispelled right now. Too often I have heard couples lament, "We can't be friends anymore. We both have changed so much. We no longer share the same interests. Our likes and dislikes are too different. We have nothing in common." What if I told you that friendship should not be based upon mutual interests, although that may initially be what brings you together. Friendship should be developed through mutual respect and admiration. Webster's 1828 Dictionary of the English Language gives an ideal description of what friendship should be.

Friendship
"An attachment to a person, proceeding from intimate acquaintance, and a reciprocation of kind offices, or from a favorable opinion of the amiable and respectable qualities of his mind....True friendship is a noble and virtuous attachment, springing from a pure source, a respect for worth or amiable qualities. False friendship...is a temporary attachment springing from interest, and may change in a moment to enmity and rancor."[21]

I found it interesting that *false* friendship was described as one "springing from interest" that could change in the blink of an eye from adoration to animosity. I thought about this in all my friendships. What were the ties that bound us together? Were my friendships based merely on commonalities? I realized that with my dearest friends, although our shared faith had brought us together, our friendship was based upon respect and admiration and that our interests varied as widely as they possibly could. I also realized that I have quite a few friends who do not share my faith at all, yet we revere each other, therefore there is a bond that holds the relationship together. Why is it then we can accept diversity in our friendships outside of our marriage yet not inside our marriage? What makes us think we want to be married to someone who only likes what we esteem? When examining the problem with friendship in marriage honestly, we will find that the friendship breaks down with a lack of respect and admiration, not because our interests as individuals have evolved.

Woody and I somewhere along the line had failed to respect each other. Romans 12:10 tells us to *"Be devoted to one another in brotherly love. Honor one another above yourselves."* We had to learn how to honor one another in order to take our relationship to the next step in intimacy, but how?

The first step requires time with God. So often our problems with honoring others stem from our lack of self-respect. Self-respect requires understanding your value in God's eyes. Do you know without a shadow of doubt God values you? You may think, "Yea, great! But you don't know the things I've done. You don't know

---

[21] Noah Webster, *American Dictionary of the English Language,* 1828, (Foundation for American Christian Education, 2006), Vol. I, 88

how I struggle with anger or bitterness or self-control. You don't see the things lurking in my past. So, that's easy for you to say. I'm a stay-at-home mom or underappreciated employee. I feel so de-valued!" Guess what. I have said all of those things. I struggle with anger control; it is a horrible demon that God has to help me battle daily, and sometimes I lose. I have been bitter. I have a past that causes me to shudder in shame anytime I recall it. I am a stay-at-home mom, and have been for seventeen years. Trust me, there have been days when I have really struggled to see the value in changing diaper after diaper, cooking, cleaning, and lending my talents as a full time taxi service. I put my education on hold in order to home educate my children, which some may think is admirable; however, in a community of women with post-graduate degrees and flourishing careers, I feel inadequate. No one is more flawed than I am. Nonetheless, God still values me just as He values you. When we spend time in God's Word and in prayer, we can't help but see our worth in God's eyes. When we come to the realization that He sent His son to suffer one of the most humiliating, horrendous deaths possible to set us free from the chains of death, how can we not feel cherished? The Bible is a love letter like no other, and you are its intended recipient. Read John 17:6-24, and insert your name in place of the pronouns "they" and "them." Do you still feel rejected? Jesus prays for your protection and sanctification. You are a highly sought after treasure. You have value! You are worthy of your spouse's respect and admiration, just as he is worthy of yours.

Once you have stepped back and spent time with God, forgiveness may be in order. Forgive your spouse for not being the person you desired. Be honest about what it is that is preventing you from accepting your spouse for whom he is, and in turn preventing you from honoring him. Often we are holding on to perceived wrongs or ideals which were not met. If there is an ongoing issue that is causing friction, deal with it quickly and specifically. Ask yourself, "Is the problem we are facing a sin issue or an expectation issue?" Many times our complaints are based upon our hopes not being met instead of broken trust or a true transgression. Once you have addressed the issue, then grant forgiveness.

When you have forgiven each other for your shortcomings, then it is time to engage in honest communication which requires really listening to each other and hearing what is being said without a critical spirit. Take fifteen minutes out of every day to sit together without interruptions (including cell phones) and acknowledge the other person's value. It may be a conversation that starts out with, "I really appreciate …. about you. I love the way you…. Tell me about …(an interest you do not share)." Spend an equal amount of time listening to each other. Be honest at all times of the day. Talk about issues as they arise, before anger sets in. I cannot tell you how many times Woody has done something to annoy me, and I have let it slide only to have it happen again and again. Then one day without any warning, I explode like Mount St. Helens spewing lava and ash all over our marriage. All the damage caused by that one eruption could have been avoided had I just said something the first time it happened. In time, you will find that these conversations which are rather forced and mechanical at the beginning will become cherished times of renewal with a dear, beloved friend. Appreciation will replace annoyance as the two of you strengthen the union that God first blessed in the Garden of Eden.

This all takes time. Do not rush the process. Only God can create a whole world in seven days. However, know that He will be slowly guiding the entire process. God told Hosea concerning Israel that He would *"lead her into the desert and speak tenderly to her."* After that Israel would no longer call Him "master" but "husband."[22] We sometimes need to be led into the desert in order to welcome the rain, but when it is all over, we are no longer feeling like slaves under a master—we are finally married to a friend. Know, too, that this will be ongoing. We cannot grow slack in protecting the friendship in marriage. It will be attacked at every angle. Put on the armor which God has provided, fighting for your friendship daily, and *"pray in the Spirit on all occasions with all kinds of prayers and requests."*[23]

It will be beneficial to explore one of the most well-known friendships in the Bible and what made it successful against all odds. Jonathan was King Saul's son and heir to rule over Israel. However, God had chosen David to do so. You would think that little detail would have been enough to discourage friendship between the two. Yet, David and Jonathan loved each other as brothers.

Read 1 Samuel 20.

David was aware of King Saul's murderous feelings. Jonathan offered to discover the truth and protect David at all costs.

---

[22] Hosea 2:14
[23] Ephesians 6:18a

How did Jonathan's actions place him in harm's way? What did he sacrifice for David?

❧ _____

_____

_____

_____

Saul hurled his spear at his own son, such was his hatred and intense jealousy of David. Jonathan protected David, sacrificing his throne in the process. Jonathan knew that God was ultimately in control; therefore, he was able to protect his friend, trusting God's will to be better than a kingdom or riches. This friendship was built on loyalty to God and to each other. Jonathan loved David as himself. I love Jonathan's last words to David, *"Go in peace, for we have sworn friendship with each other in the name of the LORD, saying, 'The LORD is witness between you and me…forever.'"*[24]

That last line sounds vaguely familiar, actually quite similar, to words spoken on my wedding day. "Dearly beloved, we are gathered here together in the presence of God and before these witnesses to join together today this man and this woman in Holy Matrimony." When we are married in most traditional Christian ceremonies, we vow with God as our witness to love sacrificially, through all circumstances—forever.

If you continue reading the story of David, you will find that in 2 Samuel 9, David had a chance to demonstrate his loyalty to Jonathan. Mephibosheth was Jonathan's lame son who had gone into hiding upon learning about King Saul's and Jonathan's deaths. David did not have to do anything for this young man. No one would have known. However, David made inquiries, discovered there was an heir, and brought Mephibosheth into his home to be treated as one of his own sons. When he had sworn friendship and allegiance to Jonathan, he had not spoken empty words. His oath had been heartfelt and lasting, just as the

---

[24] 1 Samuel 20:42

vows spoken in a marriage ceremony should be. Love survives even death. It is not circumstantial.

Another wonderful description of how we are to love one another in marriage is in Ephesians 5:22-32.

Ephesians 5:22-32

[22] Wives, submit to your husbands as to the Lord. [23] For the husband is the head of the wife as Christ is the head of the church, his body, of which he is the Savior. [24] Now as the church submits to Christ, so also wives should submit to their husbands in everything.

[25] Husbands, love your wives, just as Christ loved the church and gave himself up for her [26] to make her holy, cleansing her by the washing with water through the word, [27] and to present her to himself as a radiant church, without stain or wrinkle or any other blemish, but holy and blameless. [28] In this same way, husbands ought to love their wives as their own bodies. He who loves his wife loves himself. [29] After all, no one ever hated his own body, but he feeds and cares for it, just as Christ does the church— [30] for we are members of his body. [31] "For this reason a man will leave his father and mother and be united to his wife, and the two will become one flesh." [32] This is a profound mystery— but I am talking about Christ and the church.

According to Paul, how should a woman behave towards her husband, and likewise, how should a husband behave towards his wife?

༃ﾟ _____

_____

_____

_____

_____

Did you catch what Paul had to say in verse 33? A husband must love his wife as he loves himself, and she must respect her husband. This is a depiction of what marital friendship should be. There is nothing in this narrative about shared interest. It is all about respect and devotion.

Another passage worth reading is Proverbs 31:10-12. *"A wife of noble character who can find? She is worth far more than rubies. Her husband has full confidence in her and lacks nothing of value. She brings him good, not harm, all the days of her life."* Do you have confidence in your spouse and does he have confidence in you? Are you doing all you can to bring good into his life rather than harm? This isn't a conditional statement. There have been many times when I have felt Woody did not deserve my best. Then again, I can think of very few times when I have deserved God's best; yet that is exactly what He gave me. This is not an easy task. However, when you focus on placing your faith in God's will (just like Jonathan did) and of what He is capable, the once impossible becomes the always possible, and you will be able to love at all times.

"Father God, without Your wisdom and guidance, I cannot maneuver the path which leads to respecting the noble qualities You have placed in my spouse. Restore our friendship. Restore our admiration for each other. Give us patience as we wait for your redemptive work in our relationship. Help us to discern Your will. In Jesus' name I pray, Amen."

My Journal
continuing the journey...

date _____

CHAPTER 12

PHYSICALLY FIT FOR INTIMACY

"Thy two breasts are like two young roes that are twins, which feed among the lilies."[25] Giggles rose from the crowd of girls as the bravest one of us read aloud.

"What *are* you reading?" I queried.

"Why, the Bible." And that was my first introduction to *The Song of Solomon*. I was a fourteen year old girl at Bible camp and could not believe that something like that was in the Bible. I was confused and embarrassed and did not give the book another thought until decades later.

The Song of Solomon has been interpreted in many different ways. It has been referred to as an allegory of the love between God and Israel or between Christ and the church. Others believe it is a poetic love song about the spontaneity of love and beauty. Some believe it was written during Solomon's time on earth. Yet other biblical scholars believe it did not originate from a single author or time period. Whatever one believes concerning the meaning or authorship, there is much to be learned about God's ideal of marital love. The fact that *The Song of Solomon* is included as part of scripture is enough to know that it has relevance. "*All Scripture is God-breathed and is useful for teaching, rebuking, correcting and training in righteousness.*"[26] Even the book about sex.

God created a world full of complexities in nature and individuals; however, He also designed order into all of His creation. Physical intimacy is no exception.

---

[25] The Song of Solomon 4:5, Compact Holy Bible, Reference KJV (The Zondervan Corporation, 2000), p. 789

[26] 2 Timothy 3:16

Although every couple will experience it differently, there is a common thread that must run through every union in order to experience sex the way God intended—love and loyalty. I treat these two abstract nouns as one. You cannot have one without the other if you hope to feel the unity that is built into becoming one in the physical realm. Love and loyalty will follow spiritual and emotional intimacy. As you grow closer to God, you lean into the source of love. As you build on friendship, you learn how to be loyal. Once this is established, you are ready for physical intimacy. And although I cannot tell you what that will be like for you due to the varying nature, I can promise you that with love and loyalty it will be intimately fulfilling.

This is a very complex issue, and for no two people will it ever be the same. Your past and your spouse's past will affect your approach to this sensitive subject. The associations you both have made, whether they are beneficial or not, will determine the amount of sexual intimacy you are capable of achieving. Reaching God's potential in this area requires knowledge of God's view of marital sex. And that is the relevance of *The Song of Solomon*.

God created sex way back in the Garden of Eden. He told Adam and Eve to be fruitful and multiply. They did not have to ask God, "Uh, how do we go about doing that? You see, I have my ideas as to what 'good sex' is and she has hers. How do we meld these two ideas?" Or, "What if he doesn't satisfy me? He may not be an appropriate match. Have you noticed he's put on a little weight?" Nor did you hear Adam complain, "I'm just not physically attracted to her anymore." Obviously none of those problems existed for our ancestors. If they had, the human population could have easily gone extinct. You see, they did not have a television show telling them what defines satisfying sex or how to spice up their sex life. They did not have magazines to pour over feeding their insecurities and defining beauty for them. Most importantly, they did not have past sexual escapades in which to compare their current partner. They had each other and God.

God's continued support of marital sex is demonstrated in *The Song of Solomon*. This is a very personal, sensual book. It speaks about the exclusivity of sex. Sexual love between a husband and wife is described as powerful, pure, and precious. It also challenges young people to wait for love, being careful not to awaken or arouse it until its perfect time. The terms of endearment used between the lover and his beloved are suggestive and affectionate. Even now as a grown, married woman and mother of three, I still find my face flushes with embarrassment when I read some of the words written in this poetic masterpiece. Yet, this is the inspired Word of God included in His book. God expects married couples to have an exhilarating, satisfying sex life.

For me, this was the most difficult intimacy to restore or actually create. My history with sex—the sexual abuse and promiscuous behavior—left me with countless problems and tremendous guilt. If I enjoyed sex, I felt ashamed, as if I had done something terribly wrong. I found it challenging to be in the moment or incomprehensible as to how it could be termed "love making." Sex and love had never connected in my mind. My first experience with sex had been violent and hateful, and every experience after that had been full of betrayal and abandonment. I felt I was suffering the consequences of my sin. It had become a duty rather than a delight. No matter how I tried to separate my past from my present, I could not feel physically intimate. I had convinced myself that I did not deserve it. Perhaps if I had remained pure—if I had been one of those "good" girls—then I would be worthy enough to enjoy sex the way God purposed it to be in a covenant relationship. I was damaged property, used up, worthless. How could I ever hope to know what it felt like to encounter love through the physical act which God created?

Although you may have already closed the door on your past filled with sexual sin, sometimes it is hard to forget what is behind. You may feel as if you have crammed everything into a closet, slammed the door shut, and are standing with your back against the door just waiting for the contents to burst forth scattering filth all over your newly cleaned floors. It is easy to ask for forgiveness and accept God's grace. It is harder to shake free of the habits that have been set in place and the harmful thinking related to our pasts. The key to moving away from that closet and starting to live without guilt and fear hovering over your head is understanding that God is holding the door shut. In fact, He has cut through the wall in the back of the closet and is removing the items one by one. Pretty soon, the threat of the door bursting open will be a faint memory. He has removed your shame.

I had forgotten that. God removed my guilt and shame. He took them to the cross with Him and hung them on the tree that took His life in my place. Then He arose from the dead to prove He could overcome anything—disgrace, distress, death. He won! The battle was fought for my life, a life I could live covered by

His righteousness. All I had to do was accept it. I felt somewhat like the Israelites whom Elijah challenged on Mount Carmel, *"How long will you waver between two opinions? Is God, God or not?"*[27] Why did I struggle so hard to believe it? Why did I keep forgetting it? Why did I keep going back to the muck and mire from which He had released me?

We are so ready to believe the enemy's lies…you are not good enough…you don't deserve God's best…have you really been forgiven? We wear those foul falsehoods like medals pinned to our chest. We hide behind them and never attain the rewarding life which waits for the children of God. Stop believing the lies! You are good enough; you may not deserve God's best, but no one does—it's called grace, God's *undeserved* merit. We have all sinned, so how is your story any different from anyone who has received God's forgiveness?[28] Nonetheless, God stands by lavishing you with His absolute finest. As far as forgiveness, that is obvious. Hebrews 7:27 and Romans 6:10 clearly state Christ died to sin once and for all. This may be something you need to contemplate daily, several times a day. The more you fill your mind with God's truth, the less likely you are to believe the lies.

Once I quit wearing my badges of shame, I was able to accept God's ideal for my life. Through the Holy Bible I found a beautiful, gentle portrait of marital love and physical intimacy. God's wooing of the Israelites and Christ's wooing of the church demonstrate a patient love willing to sacrifice and serve. Our model of marriage fills the pages of the Bible. Our actions in the bedroom should mirror this gentle, giving love. I had to give myself permission to enjoy this amazing gift God has given husbands and wives. Although I had partaken of the feast before coming to the wedding banquet, God was capable of making me hungry again.

We needed a fresh start. Because of the sexual sin in our pasts, we had come together completely ill prepared to enter into a covenant relationship. We could not really promise to be faithful and become one flesh when we had already been unfaithful and had become physically united with others. Our vows had been broken before they were even spoken. As soon as I understood that, I knew it was time to go back to the beginning with a purified point of view and let God unify our union. I knew Woody and I needed to come together in purity and recommit to the covenant.

---

[27] 1 Kings 18:21
[28] Romans 3:23-24

In 1 Corinthians, Paul speaks to the church in Corinth concerning marriage. He instructs married couples regarding sexual activity, explaining that once married a wife's body belongs to her husband and vice versa. To avoid temptation, they are not to deprive each other except through mutual agreement, and then only for a time devoted to prayer.[29] This takes self-control just as remaining pure before marriage does. When a couple fails to demonstrate any restraint before marriage, they must do so afterwards. The first step in starting over is coming together and agreeing upon a time period in which to refrain from all physical intimacy. This is a physical fast from sex, which means your thoughts should not even drift in that direction. Work on developing pure thoughts about sex. Identify your weaknesses in this area and your wrong thinking. During this time, you both should be going to God in repentance for defiling God's intentions for the marriage bed and asking Him to renew your physical relationship and to restore purity to your lives. This will not be easy, but fasting from any substance is sacrifice. Prayer will give you the power needed for the time period you choose.

Throughout your physical fast, go on as many dates as you possibly can. Talk about your individual dreams and your aspirations as a couple. Set goals for your marriage. Where do you want to be as a couple in one year? Five years? Ten years? Talk about how you can demonstrate respect for one another and how you will handle situations when tempers flare. Plan for your future. Plan for the successes and failures you will experience in life. As you court each other, it will become more challenging to remain platonic, but fight the temptation. The reward will be worth the wait.

At the end of the time period you choose, go into your "tent" (bedroom) and exchange vows with each other. Include in these vows how your marriage will develop from that moment on and what you will do to preserve purity within your relationship. Then you may kiss your spouse. Consummate your marriage and know you are a new creation.

These steps are what I needed in order to feel valued again as a woman of God rather than being appreciated for the physical gratification I could provide. Since our relationship had started in the physical realm, there was always a little corner in the back of my mind piled high with feelings of doubt. Every time Woody became a little amorous, I would question, "Is this all he values me for?" The

---

[29] 1 Corinthians 7:3-5

reservations I had stemmed from the origin of our relationship. Had we built a friendship with the foundation of spiritual intimacy, I never would have had the doubts I harbored. By starting afresh with God in the forefront of our minds, I started to feel respected and loved for whom I was.

If your story is anything like mine, you need to know that there is a happy ending waiting for you, too. You can know success in this area. The battle belongs to God.

Read 1 Chronicles 5:18-22. This is the chronicle of one of the many battles the Israelites had to fight.

Who helped the Israelites during battle? Why was success given to them?

_____

_____
_____
_____
_____

The Israelites cried out to God and trusted Him. They believed with all their hearts that God would give them the victory. They knew what you need to recognize—the battle belonged to God. Do you realize that the endeavor to achieve intimacy is a battle? It is a struggle you will face on a daily basis. Do you trust God to deliver you from the enemy's attack?

I would like you to look at another verse from the history of the Israelites.

1 Kings 18:21

[21] Elijah went before the people and said, "How long will you waver between two opinions? If the Lord is God, follow him; but if Baal is God, follow him."

But the people said nothing.

In 1 Kings 18:21, what question does Elijah ask the people?

❧ _____

_____

Is God, *God* in your life? Do not cripple His power through your lack of faith. *"Is anything too hard for the Lord?"*[30] No, it is not. Give God back the power in your marriage. He does not grow tired or weary, and He is eager to give strength to those who do.[31] God is constantly aware of your struggles and misgivings. Let Him be Lord in your life. Let Him reveal the pleasures and comfort that await you when you finally relinquish control and know He alone is God.

Finally, I would like you to read aloud a few of the following passages taken from *The Song of Solomon*: 1:16-17; 2:8-14; 4:1-7, 4:11-16; 7:1-13.

Song of Solomon 1:16-17

[16] How handsome you are, my lover!

> Oh, how charming!

> And our bed is verdant.

Lover

[17] The beams of our house are cedars;

> our rafters are firs.

Song of Solomon 2:8-14

[8] Listen! My lover!

> Look! Here he comes,

leaping across the mountains,

> bounding over the hills.

---

[30] Genesis 18:14a
[31] Isaiah 40:28-29

⁹ My lover is like a gazelle or a young stag.
    Look! There he stands behind our wall,
  gazing through the windows,
    peering through the lattice.

¹⁰ My Lover spoke and said to me,
    "Arise, my darling,
    my beautiful one, and come with me.

¹¹ See! The winter is past;
    the rains are over and gone.

¹² Flowers appear on the earth;
    the season of singing has come,
  the cooing of doves
    is heard in our land.

¹³ The fig tree forms its early fruit;
    the blossoming vines spread their fragrance.
  Arise, come, my darling;
    my beautiful one, come with me."

Lover
¹⁴ My dove in the clefts of the rock,
    in the hiding places on the mountainside,
  show me your face,
    let me hear your voice;
  for your voice is sweet,
    and your face is lovely.

Song of Solomon 4:1-7

Lover

¹ How beautiful you are, my darling!
    Oh, how beautiful!
    Your eyes behind your veil are doves.
Your hair is like a flock of goats
    descending from Mount Gilead.

² Your teeth are like a flock of sheep just shorn,
    coming up from the washing,
Each has its twin;
    not one of them is alone.

³ Your lips are like a scarlet ribbon;
    your mouth is lovely.
Your temples behind your veil
    are like the halves of a pomegranate.

⁴ Your neck is like the tower of David,
    built with elegance;
on it hang a thousand shields,
    all of them shields of warriors.

⁵ Your two breasts are like two fawns,
    like twin fawns of a gazelle
    that browse among the lilies.
⁶ Until the day breaks
    and the shadows flee,

I will go to the mountain of myrrh
and to the hill of incense.

⁷ All beautiful you are, my darling;
there is no flaw in you.

Song of Solomon 4:11-16

¹¹ Your lips drop sweetness as the honeycomb, my bride;
milk and honey are under your tongue.
The fragrance of your garments is
like that of Lebanon.

¹² You are a garden locked up, my sister, my bride;
you are a spring enclosed, a sealed fountain.

¹³ Your plants are an orchard of pomegranates
with choice fruits,
with henna and nard,

¹⁴   nard and saffron,
calamus and cinnamon,
with every kind of incense tree,
with myrrh and aloes
and all the finest spices.

¹⁵ You are a garden fountain,
a well of flowing water
streaming down from Lebanon.

Beloved

¹⁶ Awake, north wind,
> and come, south wind!

Blow on my garden,
> that its fragrance may spread abroad.

Let my lover come into his garden
> and taste its choice fruits.

Song of Solomon 7:1-13

¹ How beautiful your sandaled feet,
> O prince's daughter!

Your graceful legs are like jewels,
> the work of a craftsman's hands.

² Your navel is a rounded goblet
> that never lacks blended wine.

Your waist is a mound of wheat
> encircled by lilies.

³ Your breasts are like two fawns,
> twins of a gazelle.

⁴ Your neck is like an ivory tower.

Your eyes are the pools of Heshbon
> by the gate of Bath Rabbim.

Your nose is like the tower of Lebanon
> looking toward Damascus.

⁵ Your head crowns you like Mount Carmel.
　　Your hair is like royal tapestry;
　　the king is held captive by its tresses.

⁶ How beautiful you are and how pleasing,
　　O love, with your delights!

⁷ Your stature is like that of the palm,
　　and your breasts like clusters of fruit.

⁸ I said, "I will climb the palm tree;
　　I will take hold of its fruit."
　May your breasts be like the clusters of the vine,
　　the fragrance of your breath like apples,

⁹　　and your mouth like the best wine.

Beloved

May the wine go straight to my lover,
　　flowing gently over lips and teeth.

¹⁰ I belong to my lover,
　　and his desire is for me.

¹¹ Come, my lover, let us go to the countryside,
　　let us spend the night in the villages.

¹² Let us go early to the vineyards
>   to see if the vines have budded,
> if their blossoms have opened,
>   and if the pomegranates are in bloom—
> there I will give you my love.

¹³ The mandrakes send out their fragrance,
>   and at our door is every delicacy,
> both new and old,
>   that I have stored up for you, my lover.

What is the love like between this bride and groom?

_____
_____
_____
_____
_____

This is some of the most intimate language recorded for our benefit. Who needs a Harlequin romance novel when you have stuff like this? If you have never read this little gem in the Bible, I suggest you do so with your husband. Let him read the part of the lover while you read the part of the beloved. Be inspired by the stimulating language of this lovely poem, and know that God wants you to experience the same tender, passionate love-making that this couple knew on their wedding night. Let your desire be for each other. Find the flawless beauty in a love built on the foundation of faith, strengthened by the emotional bonds of friendship, and sealed in the sweet, pure love-making which can only be experienced within a covenant relationship.

God can awaken your appetite for the pleasures your spouse has to provide and those that you have to contribute. He will remove your guilt and give you permission to find fulfillment within the protective bonds of marriage. Soon you too may speak as the beloved in *The Song of Solomon* speaks of her lover, and you will know without doubt that *"My lover is mine and I am his."*[32]

Guard your thoughts as you journey towards this place of pleasure. It will not be comparable to the lies you have been offered daily by a society obsessed with sex. However, try to remember that God's ideal is far superior to any the world may offer, although it may take time to discover it.

My prayer is that as you have traveled through this book, you have been travelling towards intimacy. However, your journey is not over, it has just begun. This is an ongoing voyage with pot holes and hurdles around every corner. Yet every step of the way, our wonderful God stands ready to pick you up, dust you off, and send you on always pointing you in the direction of success. We do not make this trek alone. At times we are led and at others we are carried. And always we are loved.

Intimacy—something I have sought for nearly 40 years—has been waiting for me in the arms of my Savior. If only I had known it begins with Him (as we find spiritual intimacy) and ends with Him (as we enter into physical intimacy), perhaps the journey would not have taken so long. However, now that I know where to look, I will never be lost again. My marriage is a living testament to God's transformational power. The voyage was severe—nearly fatal to our relationship. However, now we are at the summit and the view is breathtaking! The air is clear. The breathing is easy. I am praying that you too will never be led astray. Stay the course. Continue climbing and you will discover unimaginable treasures. Press on, for intimacy is the prize to be found at the end of the road.

---

[32] Song of Songs 2:16

*"Father God, so many steps have been taken
down the road which leads to intimacy.
I know there are so many more to be taken.
I pray that You will take my hand and
lead me every second of every day. With You,
all things are possible. Give me permission
to love and be loved, to trust and be trusted.
Let me be a blessing to the wonderful person
to whom You joined me.
In Jesus 'holy name I pray, Amen."*

My Journal

continuing the journey...

date _____

www.ingramcontent.com/pod-product-compliance
Lightning Source LLC
Chambersburg PA
CBHW060832050426
42453CB00008B/668